THE COMPLETE
ENTREPRENEUR

THE COMPLETE ENTREPRENEUR

A Guide to Survival for the Small Business

David Oates

MERCURY BOOKS
Published by W.H. Allen & Co Plc

First published in 1987
by the Mercury Books Division of
W.H. Allen & Co. Plc
44 Hill Street, London W1X 8LB

Set in Concorde by Phoenix Photosetting, Chatham
Printed and bound in Great Britain by
Mackays of Chatham Ltd, Chatham, Kent

British Library Cataloguing in Publication Data

Oates, David
    The complete entrepreneur: a guide to
    survival for the small business.
    1. Small business——Great Britain——
    Management
    I. Title
    658'.022'0941   HD62.7

    ISBN 1–85251–010–2

FOREWORD

After spending most of my career as a business journalist
writing about how big companies around the world are managed, I decided about six years ago to specialise on docu-
menting the successes and failures of small businesses in
Britain. The transition from the macro to the micro has been
a fascinating one.

Big companies and small businesses live in different
worlds. Big companies tend to operate from prestigious
corporate head offices, have an infinite amount of resources
and money often seems no object when setting out to achieve
their goals. By contrast, small businesses are usually run from
remote, sparsely-furnished workshops, have very limited
resources and often don't know where the next penny is
coming from to keep the operation ticking over. While big
company moguls are surrounded by a retinue of advisers, the
small business entrepreneur usually has to make do with the
minimum of support staff and leads a lonely existence with
few to share his troubles.

When it is considered that this is supposed to be the age of
the small business and that it is the small business entre-

preneur on whom Britain is largely pinning its hopes for economic recovery, he is still a surprisingly beleaguered individual. Hardly a day passes without some government spokesman announcing a new measure to help the small businessman in his struggle for survival. Judging from TV and newspaper advertisements, the big high street banks are falling over each other in their attempts to oil the financial wheels of small businesses. Local councils and dozens of enterprise agencies, run by well-intentioned administrators, shower their benevolent services on small businesses, willing them to succeed.

Yet, despite all this apparent support, many small business entrepreneurs feel they are a neglected breed and that they are fighting a lone battle it is almost impossible for them to win. They are beset by problems. Raising capital from banks and venture capitalists seems to be an uphill battle, to say the least. Many small firms have insufficient financial resources to hire in badly needed expertise or to invest in new technology. They cannot afford to indulge in expensive marketing schemes to get their products known. They are swamped with government red tape and they often have to wait an inordinate length of time to get paid for the goods and services they supply.

With so much to contend with, it is hardly surprising so many small business start-ups never make it. What is surprising is that there seems to be a never-ending stream of volunteers with the courage to take up the challenge of trying to create a company that with a certain amount of good fortune and a great deal of dedication might become part of the fabric of tomorrow's industrial scene.

It was with the idea of helping the growth of the small business sector that this book was conceived. In visiting hundreds of small business entrepreneurs during the course of my journalistic pursuits, compiling case study features for the local and national press, I have found myself becoming something of a champion of their cause – something that never happened to me when writing about blue chip companies.

It is almost impossible, if you spend a number of years writing about small firms, not to become infected with the missionary zeal that most entrepreneurs seem to generate. It is of course a bad thing for a journalist to become emotionally involved in his subject matter. But in seeking the universal lessons that have been learned by Britain's comparatively young generation of small business entrepreneurs I have found myself joining the ranks of those anxious to see them succeed.

There is now a veritable army of people and organisations in Britain trying to spur on entrepreneurial endeavour. An enormous number of advisers have also contributed to the contents of this book. I should like to thank in particular Colin Breed, a director of merchant bankers Dartington & Co., for sparing the time to debate the problems of raising finance, and Albert Johnston of the East Devon Small Industries Group, Colin Bradley of the Small Firms Service, marketing consultant Ian Jennings and Judith Bloor, publisher of *Your Business* magazine for their invaluable inputs. The Council for Small Industries in Rural Areas (CoSIRA) has been extremely helpful in the effort to track down exemplary small businesses. I am most grateful of all to the hundreds of small business entrepreneurs who have been willing to tell their story so that others who follow in their wake may be that little bit wiser.

DAVID OATES

CONTENTS

1

THE WOULD-BE ENTREPRENEUR

ENTERING a new market was an important development for the company and the directors sitting around the boardroom table became animated as they discussed the strategy they should adopt.

Ideas were bandied around, debated, adopted and dismissed, until finally a plan of attack emerged and the meeting broke up.

A familiar scene at companies all over the world, but this was a meeting with a difference. The directors were all teenagers and, perhaps most surprising of all, they were all female.

The meeting was not taking place in the plush boardroom of a major corporation in one of the nation's industrial centres. It was being conducted in a cramped common room at a private school for girls and all the 'directors' were schoolchildren.

Yet is was no game they were playing. The mini-company they were running mirrored in every respect the cut and thrust of the real commercial world. The company raised capital by issuing shares (mainly to parents and friends), made products, marketed them, paid wages and aimed to make a profit at the end of the day to be paid out in the form of a dividend.

The company was typical of hundreds of similar ventures being run all over Britain under the Young Enterprise Scheme, which was set up as an educational charity to provide practical business experience to thousands of young people between the ages of fifteen and nineteen.

It is a heartening sign that educationalists at long last see the merits of familiarising young people with the principles of the free enterprise system at the earliest opportunity. The ingenious scheme is symptomatic of the entrepreneurial spirit currently sweeping Britain. Children are being taught how to become entrepreneurs because of a realisation that it is a way of life that is going to play an increasingly important role in the national economy and in our future society.

The age of enterprise has arrived. Britain can no longer be described as a nation of shopkeepers. It is now a nation of entrepreneurs, albeit mainly small business entrepreneurs.

Many factors combine to make the time ripe for such a development; not least the all-pervasive changes being triggered by the post-industrial society. Automation and information technology are causing a swing away from manufacturing towards the service industries. Many of the services increasingly in demand are better provided by small autonomous units rather than by huge monolithic corporations.

The traditional manufacturing firms with their roots in the industrial past, are being forced to rationalize as automation takes over from manpower. Employees are being shed in their thousands and are finding themselves with little prospect of alternative employment.

The post-industrial society is also causing the whole structure of our economic institutions to come under review. Latest technology is challenging the sense of huge masses of people gathering in concentrated locations to perform industrial tasks. The traditional rigid command structures, based on church and military hierarchies, are giving way to more loose-knit, informal systems. Flexi-hours are merging into flexi-years and flexi-lives.

Increasingly, people are seeing the advantages of doing their own thing, in their own way, in their own time. Entrepreneurs can control their own lives, structure their own progress and be answerable for their own achievements.

The development is being spurred on by government which sees that the only real prospect of economic growth and job creation is through a proliferation of small businesses striving to make a go of it.

At some stage in their lives, most people have nursed a secret ambition to set up their own business. Until recently, however, relatively few had been prepared to exchange the security of employment for the precarious uncertainty of a high-risk venture.

It is all too easy to find excuses for putting off the fatal moment and to allow the ambition to become nothing more than a pipe-dream. It is the wrong time for the family; there is a heavy mortgage to pay and nothing should prevent the children from receiving a good education.

Or it can be argued that your career is progressing well; let things ride a few more years and you will have built up valuable experience that will stand you in good stead when you finally take the plunge.

At the other end of the scale is the saddest excuse of all. You only have ten years to go before you receive your company pension. Why throw away all those years of sweat and toil for what could easily be an abortive exercise?

Today, however, many of those who would probably never have taken those first faltering steps towards going it alone are being precipitated into action. As the major companies contract, driven by the inexorable march of technological progress, many who would probably have remained company men all their lives are suddenly confronted with no alternative but to become self-employed and masters of their own fate.

Redundancy is a marvellous spur to action. There is no longer any excuse for vacillation. The reality is stark and menacing. The prospect of finding another job comparable to the one that has been lost is remote. The only way to retain any vestige of dignity and earn enough to maintain the customary standard of living is to turn that vague ambition to go it alone some day into a concrete plan for the immediate future.

Not everyone who starts a new business does so because they have been made redundant, of course, or because they find the idea of being on the dole repugnant. A lot of would-be entrepreneurs have simply waited until they have felt equal to the task. The mid-forties is a favourite time, when the children are beginning to fly the nest and the repercussions of failure are likely to be less devastating. It may be that the would-be entrepreneur feels he has accumulated enough experience from working for somebody else to cope with the demands of running his own operation.

Others become entrepreneurs to get out of the rat race. They may have become disenchanted with corporate life and the internal politics it invariably involves. Or they may simply have started to question the value of blind career ambition and where it is leading them. There are growing signs that getting to the top of a corporation is losing its appeal. The alternative of running your own show and being in control of your own future is becoming ever more attractive, particularly as it also often provides the freedom to live in an environmentally pleasant part of the country.

Mid-career drop-outs are only one source to fuel the new-found entrepreneurial spirit in Britain. An increasing number of young people are starting up their own businesses straight from school or college, many of them encouraged by the government's Enterprise Allowance Scheme, which provides them with £40 a week for the first year of the operation. These young people, with the freshness and vigour of youth, often make surprisingly successful entrepreneurs.

Inevitably, with such a klondike rush to join the ranks of the small business entrepreneurs, the fall-out rate is high. Nationally, it has been estimated that one in three new start-ups never reach their third year. Hundreds are forced into liquidation every year and many more throw in the towel.

With the odds so heavily stacked against success it is perhaps surprising that there is no sign of a slow-down in the flood of people deciding to go it alone. For many it is a pragmatic decision, often inspired by a determination to preserve a way of life that is under threat.

When a major food group decided to pull out of the bread business because of an over-capacity in the market, the seven managers at one of its regional bakeries were reluctant to see the company they had built up vanish overnight. They could not afford to buy the bakery outright, but they decided to prove that the business could still be made viable by starting their own company. They reasoned that a small, independent bakery would not be constrained by the same economies of scale sought by bigger groups. The alternative to taking this daring step was to move away from a part of the country in which they all enjoyed living to find jobs elsewhere. They were determined not to let that happen.

To help raise the capital for the venture, the former managers even undertook the tender to demolish the former bakehouse. In setting up their own company, they realized they needed to offer their customers something special to lure them away from the big league bakery firms with famous brand names.

They went back to the old style of producing loaves from a slow, twenty-five minute mix, which resulted in a crisp, wholesome loaf. They also introduced a successful range of

[5]

high-fibre wholemeal breads just when health foods were becoming all the vogue.

But their real breakthrough came when they introduced a loaf based on a recipe originating from the remote kingdom of Turkestan, where the locals have been known to live to the ripe old age of 150. The Turkestan loaf was an instant success and sales soared all over the country. When they first went into business for themselves, the directors had anticipated a sales turnover of around £11,000 a week, but it soon surpassed all their expectations by rising to £30,000 a week. Before long they were achieving an annual turnover of several million pounds.

The bakery directors were comforted by the knowledge that however great the risk they were taking, it was shared between the seven of them. More often, however, it is a lone hero who comes to the aid of an ailing firm, bringing him his first encounter with the daunting prospect of becoming a small business entrepreneur.

Such was the experience of Simon Unwin. Several years ago, when the recession was hitting the boating industry hard, the small sail-making firm he was working for could easily have joined the ranks of business failures. But Unwin, who had joined the firm as a sail-maker and had worked his way up to become second in command to the firm's owner, was unprepared to let it founder.

After a loss-making period, the firm's owner had made up his mind to move on to other things. He had already prepared redundancy notices for his staff when Unwin stepped in to rescue the firm from oblivion. Trained as an accountant, Unwin was convinced that with a certain amount of judicial pruning, the firm could be made profitable again. He drew up a turnaround plan and approached the bank and the Council for Small Industries in Rural Areas (CoSIRA) for loans that would allow him to purchase the company from its founder.

The total salvage package to put the wind back in the

company's sails amounted to £25,000, most of which Unwin obtained under the government's loan guarantee scheme. His main strategy was to cut overheads and reduce the amount of production space, saving rent and heating costs. He also cut back on advertising in expensive yachting magazines, convinced that the high quality of the craftsmanship in the company's sails spoke for itself.

The turnaround was not dramatic, but on a steady turnover of £100,000 a year, Unwin was at least able to fulfil his main aims of bailing out the sail company and preserving a way of life he was reluctant to let go. 'I learned to sail from my father when I was about ten and have always loved it. If I had stuck to some of the other jobs I have had in my life I would probably be a lot better off than I am now, but I wouldn't be enjoying life half so much', he explained simply.

There are many other reasons company men are catapulted into becoming entrepreneurs. Sometimes it is because a company is unwilling to back an idea an employee is convinced is a certain market winner. While working for the UK subsidiary of a major West German chemical group, Robert Mann stumbled on an idea for a fire protection product he was sure would sell well.

The idea was based on an intumescent material which expands under heat, sealing off the weakest points in doors and other structures and preventing fires from spreading. Mann saw great potential in the idea and tried to persuade the chemical group, which already produced the basic material, to turn it into a finished product that could be incorporated in door structures.

But the chemical group did not see sufficient prospects for the product idea. It felt the product was too specialized and unlikely to generate big enough sales volumes to justify the necessary investment.

Mann's confidence was unshaken, particularly as the development coincided with the introduction of stricter fire precautions in Britain. He had long nursed the idea of starting his own business and decided to branch out on his own. 'I realized that if you could marry up this intumescent material with a PVC extrusion you would have a very saleable product', he recalled.

The chemical group gave Mann its full support to start his own business, but he became an entrepreneur with some trepidation. 'I had a lot of misgivings about leaving the firm because I had a very secure job and it was a wonderful company to work for', he said. 'The firm agreed to supply me with the raw material at a good price and helped me with credit. We have maintained a very close relationship with the company since.

'I had always wanted to run my own business, but I was sensible enough to realize that you had to have a good product you could sell day in and day out. I felt I had been presented with this opportunity and that if I didn't take it I would always regret it. Of course, I had a shop window on what was happening in the market, because I could see so many people wanting the finished product and being turned away and told they would have to process the raw material themselves.'

Mann's gamble paid off. Within five years he had built the idea into a company with a £400,000 turnover with exports to a host of countries, including the Middle East, Australia and Japan.

It is not only company men who set up in business as a result of disenchantment with corporate life. Professional people, too, often see private enterprise as the way to end frustrations in their career development.

Clint Thrippleton, a former head teacher of a county primary school, dreamed of the day when education could be something more than learning out of books and lectures in the classroom. In particular, he felt there was tremendous scope for bringing teaching alive through educational trips to famous cities and sites steeped in history.

'What is called an educational visit is often just dumping children at a field centre for five days. With the best will in the world, teachers don't have the resources or the time to organize visits properly', Thrippleton concluded.

Rather than just ponder on what might have been, he decided to to something about it. He left behind the cloistered academic world and immersed himself in the world of hard business reality setting up a company together with a friend, a former marketing manager.

The company they founded was basically a travel agency for schoolchildren, but more than that, it provided all the educational aids to make visits to places of historic interest, like York and Bath, more exciting. Thrippleton's company created a veritable Aladdin's cave of educational aids, ranging from construction kits for making model Elizabethan houses and prehistoric animals and brass rubbing equipment to imitation Roman coins and beautifully illustrated books on architecture and other colourful subjects.

Thrippleton succeeded in turning a bright idea into a flourishing business that satisfied his own desires to see education made more vivid and which at the same time filled a market need by taking the slog out of school trips for overworked teachers.

One of the most popular routes to self-employment is via a management buy-out, where managers raise the capital to purchase a business or division from their company, which they then run independently. It has several distinct advantages. The business, which is already a going concern, stays in the hands of the managers who built it up. They will continue to run a company with which they already feel familiar and comfortable rather than launching an unknown quantity. The parent group, for its part, is only too happy to see the division it is anxious to shed handed over to former employees. It eases the conscience and avoids the trauma of announcing redundancies.

[9]

The buy-out frenzy of recent years has been fuelled by the venture capitalists who have been drawn like moths to a candle at the prospect of investing in a low-risk sector of the business market. One estimate puts the total annual UK market in buy-outs at around £1 billion and there are few signs of it slowing down.

Venture capitalists are attracted by management buy-outs because it means investing in a management team with a proven track record. Citicorp's venture capital arm, for instance, rarely invests in a new start-up unless there is a complete management team in place.

The big attraction of the buy-out boom, observes a director of Citicorp Venture Capital Ltd., is that 'you're getting more experienced management and better quality management prepared to take risks, which wasn't the case a few years ago. There's an awareness now that instead of working for a large industrial company for the rest of one's life and being concerned about pension rights, managers can personally earn a lot of money in a very short period of time by participating in a buy-out'.

What appeals to Citicorp is that those seeking its financial backing in a buy-out situation are 'currently managing the business, in some cases very successfully'.

The somewhat depressing fact of life for small businesses at the lower end of the scale, however, is that venture capital firms tend not to be interested in investments below the £250,000 mark. Citicorp's average investment is around £800,000.

Other investors, such as 3i (Investors in Industry) and some of the clearing banks, including Midland Equity Capital, are prepared to invest smaller amounts, however. But most argue that it costs as much to set up and monitor a small buy-out as it does a large one.

Management buy-outs nevertheless look like being one of the favourite routes to self-employment for some time to come. In many cases the parent company does not decide to dispose of a division because it is inherently unsuccessful. It may simply be the result of a corporate decision to rationalize or to hive off businesses which no longer fit into the overall business strategy.

Set loose to be run as a separate entity, however, the division may well prosper without the constraints imposed on it by the former parent group. From the motivational point of view, the former managers, now turned entrepreneurs, are more likely to put extra effort into a venture that has their own capital riding on it.

A prime example of this is Tiverton Fabrications Ltd., a company that used to be part of Northern Engineering Industries (NEI), based in Gateshead. Formerly known as Weldcontrol, the Tiverton firm used to make welding equipment for the nuclear industry. In 1982, NEI, which at the time had an annual turnover of around £650 million and 23,000 employees worldwide, set Weldcontrol an annual sales target of £1.2 million. The Tiverton firm was unable to meet the target, largely because of foreign competition. NEI decided to close it down and absorb its activities into another part of the group.

But two managers and four shopfloor workers who had been working for the Tiverton firm were not prepared to see the hard work they had invested in the company swallowed up in a rationalisation programme. They wasted no time in mounting a rescue plan. Within eight weeks they had bought the fabrication equipment from NEI with £25,000 under a government-guranteed bank loan and £15,000 out of their own pockets, most of it redundancy money.

Although it was business as usual at the firm, Peter Nickels, the former projects manager, who was elected chairman of the new company, noted a significant change in the way the company was run.

'You have a totally different attitude to work,' he observed.

'You work much harder and you're always conscious of costs. You switch off the lights and make telephone calls in the afternoon, which you wouldn't bother to do when you're working for someone else. You realize every time you do something, it's your money you're spending'.

Not every aspiring entrepreneur wants to start up a business that is simply a continuation of what he had been doing before. The Carpenters Workshop, a company that supplies wooden kitchen and bathroom accessories to such leading stores as Marks & Spencer, was founded by three former directors from the food industry. None of them had even so much as nailed two pieces of wood together before. But they were motivated by the challenge of starting up in a sector of the market, of which they had no previous experience. It proved no handicap in creating a business which was soon enjoying an annual turnover of millions of pounds.

'Our lack of experience was probably our greatest asset,' suggested Richard Martin, one of the founding directors. 'In an industry that is noted for its conservatism and backward thinking, we have managed to carve out a bit of a success for ourselves, because we have tended to take a different approach to the way manufacturers have historically operated.'

Some have to accept, however, that they are so steeped in a particular industry that they would be courting disaster if they stepped outside it. It is far safer sticking to their last. Raymond Cleeve, for instance, was made redundant from Van Heusen, the leading shirt manufacturers, over a decade ago. He hunted in vain for another job and toyed with the idea of going in for something entirely different.

But he finally concluded he was cut out for one thing only – making shirts. The answer was to set up his own company, but he knew from the start that he would not be able to compete with the mass production firms unless he offered something different. So he decided to produce high-quality shirts for up-market customers. To ensure that his shirts met the high requirements of such a demanding market, he introduced the technique of quality circles, under which his factory workers inspect their own craftsmanship.

The technique was originally devised for the highly sensitive aerospace industries in the US and Japan, but Cleeve found the principles equally applicable to shirt-making. As well as ensuring good quality workmanship, the approach involved Cleeve's workforce deeply in the progress of the business and increased their motivation. As a result, he found a ready market for his stylish shirts in leading West End men's wear shops.

A change of personal circumstances can be the spark that sets an aspiring entrepreneur on the small business trail. Johanna Sheen was spurred into action when her husband announced he intended to give up his lucrative job as an advertising executive to attend a fulltime course at the London Business School. She knew she was going to have to do something urgently to supplement their income. The grant her husband would receive towards the course would fall far short of supporting the standard of living to which they had grown accustomed.

Johanna decided the answer was to start her own business, but she had a very young baby daughter, so it had to be a product line she could produce from home. After several abortive experiments she discovered her forte. It was making pictures from pressed flowers grown in her garden, which she managed to turn into a thriving business. Her original designs in elegant picture frames eventually sold in their thousands in Harrods and other leading stores. She also opened up a flourishing export business.

Trade became so brisk her husband later joined her in the venture, rejecting any thought of going back into advertising.

Right from childhood, Pauline Ralph had enjoyed making things, usually from scraps of wood with a cheap fret saw.

When she eventually had children of her own, she delighted them with the dolls houses and model farms she made. By the time her children had grown into teenagers, she began to think of how she might turn her toy-making skills into a viable business.

She finally hit on the idea of making thatched cottage musical boxes. The original design has since spawned forty-five different cottage models that sell all over the world and bring in the Ralphs a turnover of close to £1 million a year.

The business has become so successful, Pauline's husband eventually left the security of his job as managing director of a leading textile firm to join her full time in the enterprise.

Pauline Ralph is typical of a new breed of women entre-preneurs with bright ideas and the tenacity to see them imple-mented, who are determined to exchange the drudgery of the kitchen sink for the exhilaration of commercial enterprise. But not all women who set up in business do so because their children have flown the nest and they are searching for some-thing stimulating to fill their days.

When Valerie Burrell re-married, she felt it unfair to expect her second husband to finance the education of her children from her first marriage. A keen home knitter, it occurred to her she might be able to raise the necessary funds by turning her hobby into a cottage industry. She advertised for out-workers and six like-minded women applied and provided the nucleus of a business that was eventually recording an annual turnover of hundreds of thousands of pounds.

Some people become small business entrepreneurs by accident. Isabel Griffiths is a good example. She had always been good at needlework and was asked by a friend to repair the cushion the pet cat used to lie on. Rather than repair the worn-out cushion, Isabel made a completely new one. She made such a good job of it, her friend asked if she would make a spare.

Other friends and relatives admired her handiwork and

before she knew it there was a constant demand for the pet cushions. Isabel's husband took note of his wife's success and decided as an academic exercise to tour local pet shops to find out whether there would be a ready market for the cushions. He was left in no doubt that there would be a strong demand for them.

The couple formed a company that ended up selling pet products all over the world. They built up the range to include dog baskets and pet clothing, such as tartan dog jackets and lamé knickers bought by wealthy US dog owners seeking sartorial elegance for their pet poodles.

Nobody was more surprised to find herself running a company than Deborah Maurer, who ended up, through a similar set of unpredictable circumstances, marketing a zither-like instrument imported from the Ukraine.

She was originally given the instrument, known as a cimbala, by a friend. After failing to teach her young son to play it properly, she invented a system of musical notation, which did away with bothersome crotchets and semi-quavers.

Deborah, a maths teacher by profession, simply placed dots on a sheet of paper under the strings at the spot where they should be plucked. Her son found, to his delight, that he could instantly strike up a recognizable tune.

A number of intrigued friends and relatives badgered Deborah to obtain cimbalas for them and for six months she searched for an import house prepared to arrange transportation across the vast plains of Russia from the Ukraine to the port of Leningrad.

She had to part with her life savings and knock down the importers from an initial order of 500 to 120 cimbalas to get the ball rolling. It wasn't until a large pile of crates were delivered to her home that Deborah fully realized what she had let herself in for. 'I could just about lift them into a wheel-barrow and carry them into my cottage,' she remembered with amusement.

[15]

But Deborah didn't need to do any advertising to dispose of the instruments. They sold like hot cakes. At the end of the exercise, she had made a small profit and the idea gradually dawned on her that perhaps she had stumbled on a new outlet for her energies. 'I suddenly thought that maybe I was actually supposed to be doing this for the next ten or twenty years of my life,' she recalled.

Niels Svendsen is someone else who became an entrepreneur almost by accident. He was so impressed with the performance of an energy saving device he had installed in the hotel he was running that he decided to form a company to market the idea.

The unit, based on the concept of combined heat and power (CHP), provided electricity for a new wing of the hotel and at the same time heated the water in the swimming pool. Svendsen was convinced that the idea should be adopted more widely by hotels, hospitals and industry. The savings, he envisaged, could be tremendous.

He estimated, for example, that if all the hotels in Britain installed CHP units, the energy saved would be equivalent to the output of two nuclear power stations.

Svendsen had little idea he would become so sold on CHP when he explored the idea of installing a small unit called Totem, based on the engine of a Fiat 125, in his hotel. At the time, he was planning a twelve-bedroom extension and the electricity board told him his existing power supply would have to be reinforced by putting in new power lines at a cost of around £5,000.

By coincidence, a salesman called at the hotel at around about the same time offering the Totem unit for roughly the same cost. But in addition to generating electricity, the water used for cooling the engine would heat the hotel swimming pool.

The system in fact worked so well it generated surplus electricity, fed power back into the grid causing the hotel's electricity meter to run in reverse. In addition to all the other advantages, Svendsen had stumbled on a way to reduce the hotel's electricity bill. He needed no further encouragement to set up a company to market Totem and much larger units ranging up to 155kWs.

Britain's small business entrepreneurs certainly don't lack ingenuity when it comes to selecting a product line to start up in. There are of course large numbers of small businessmen successfully making a living from selling run-of-the-mill products. But in today's highly competitive economic climate, the entrepreneur who enters the market with a slightly off-beat product or service starts with a distinct advantage.

One man who has never had a lot of competition is Michael Davies, an affable Welshman in his sixties, who makes a living from hammering out suits of armour, ranging in style from the time of Phillip II of Spain to the Black Prince.

Surprisingly, in the nuclear age, there is still a heavy demand for medieval armour. Davies' creations go all over the world to such unlikely places as Finland, Iceland and Saudi Arabia. They are used by interior designers, in shops, pubs and hotels and by companies looking for an advertising gimmick.

Davies takes pride in getting as close to the original designs as he can, even to the extent of eschewing modern production methods. The only concession he makes to modern times is a steel roller that is wound by hand, like a primitive mangle.

He even overcame the problem of making the armour look ancient. 'We have a process that accelerates age,' he explained in his workshop, cluttered with half-completed visors, shields and swords. 'It's really quite an art to make steel look as though it's hundreds of years old. We have to treat it with a mild corrosive and leave it to age until it looks genuinely old.'

When visitors to Devon stop for bed and breakfast at the rambling farm house near Totnes belonging to Michael and Angela Cox, they sleep in the grandeur of a fourposter bed. Some of them fall in love with the idea and end up buying a fourposter bed for their own home.

In a workshop adjoining the farm house, Michael Cox turns out about two fourposters a month based on nine different designs, ranging from 15th century Elizabethan models to reproductions of Chippendales and Hepplewhites. They sell not only to customers who have sampled the comforts of the farm's bed and breakfast facilities, but to people living as far afield as Canada, Bermuda and America. He has even had inquiries from Africa.

Surprisingly, many of his orders come not from the owners of ancestral estates, but from young couples setting up home. It has become highly fashionable for newly-weds to install fourposters in their first homes. Cox attributes the demand to a reaction to the high divorce rate. Couples are looking for something solid to anchor their marriage to, he suggests. And you can't get anything much more solid than a mahogany fourposter, draped with brocade.

When Julian Sharples graduated from Durham University with a good engineering degree, he was convinced he had been handed a ticket for life-long employment. But after months of job-searching, he couldn't find any work that offered him any kind of a challenge.

Instead he set up a company with two other Durham graduates that creates catchy jingles for TV and radio commercials. Julian freely admits it was an enormous gamble, as none of them had any business experience or knew the first thing about keeping accounts.

One thing they were confident about was that they could compose better jingles than the bland tunes they heard being pumped monotonously out of commercial radio stations every day.

Operating at first from home and later above a recording studio in Manchester, they minimized the risk by keeping their overheads low. 'We bought some letterheads and went out into the world and pretended we were a company – and people believed us,' recalled Julian, amused by their audacity. 'We hold out a ray of hope for people who are in the same position we were in when we left college. Half the people in my year didn't get jobs when they left Durham.'

With a hair style that would make Bob Geldof envious and dressed in a jazzy, check jacket, Julian is hardly the epitome of the conventional managing director. But after attending a course on how to run a small business at the London Enterprise Agency, he has seen his company grow from strength to strength.

Some entrepreneurs create new opportunities by taking a novel approach to traditional markets. You could hardly think of a more mundane product than the humble sandwich. But the Brown family of Battersea, who deliver sandwiches to hungry office dwellers all over London, do things in style.

Their delivery boys cycle through the back streets of London wearing deer-stalker hats and quaint knee-breeches, bringing a little colour into the grey world of busy executives. The bicycles negotiate London's traffic-clogged streets with ease. The style of dress reinforces the image the company, appropriately named Rumbly Tummy Fillers, has been building up over the years for good old-fashioned service coupled with good quality food.

All the sandwiches are made from wholemeal bread and filled with natural food products prepared in a spotless kitchen at the converted Battersea railway arch that serves as the company's headquarters. They even make the mayonnaise for the sandwiches from free-range eggs sent up specially from Wiltshire.

Alan Brown, one of three brothers in the family business

started by their mother, finds the old-fashioned approach works wonders. Most people, he discovered early on, have an in-built resistance to salesmen, but his Victorian style dress helps to break the ice.

'The deer-stalker reminds them of Sherlock Holmes and they instantly warm to me,' he said cheerfully. 'They also associate old-fashioned things with good quality and health – with the times before additives and hormones were introduced into food. People smile when they see me ride by, which is rare these days.

'It's integral to our approach. We're not just in the business of flogging sandwiches and making as much money as we can. Obviously, making money is important, but we are trying to offer people a pleasant way of life.'

Whatever route the budding entrepreneur chooses to enter the business world, it takes an enormous amount of resilience to see his plans realized. Practically every small businessman will tell you that he went through sheer hell in the first two years and that if he had known what he was letting himself in for, he would probably never have embarked on self-employment.

Most small business entrepreneurs can reel off an endless stream of horror stories about events that brought them close to bankruptcy. Not everyone has the consititution to ride out such potential disasters, particularly if they have come from the comparatively sheltered world of a protective big company.

There has been a lot of research carried out by behavioural scientists as to whether people can change their personalities to suit different circumstances. It is theoretically possible for someone who has been a company man most of his life to switch horses in mid-career and discover he has the psychological make-up to become that very different animal – the entrepreneur. But there is a strongly-held view abroad that the really successful entrepreneurs are made in heaven – that no form of training can turn a company man into a self-motivating visionary.

Becoming a small business entrepreneur undoubtedly calls upon inner resources to which some people have more ready access than others. Ask any entrepreneur what qualities most helped him to survive the early years and the reply will be something along the lines of 'bloodymindedness', 'determination verging on paranoia' or 'refusal to be beaten'.

Those who run courses for people planning to start their own business tend at the outset to stress the sheer grind involved and leave the participants in little doubt that they must need their heads examined to even contemplate the idea. They also usually emphasize that it is important to become an entrepreneur for the right reasons. It isn't simply enough to decide to start up a business because you have been made redundant.

That might be the spark that finally ignites the entrepreneurial desire, but it is not a reason in itself. The main factor should be that you feel you have what it takes to build up a company against severe odds and that the exhilaration you will get from the achievement will outweigh the hardships you will undoubtedly have to endure.

It is probably true to say that nobody really knows what inner resources they possess until they are put to the test, but the most successful entrepreneurs are likely to be those who have harboured the idea of going it alone for some time and have just been waiting for the right opportunity to come along. They will already have become mentally attuned to the possibility and will have built up over a period of time a psychological readiness for combat which those plunged into the fray on the spur of the moment will almost certainly lack.

The heartbreaking experience of Robert Meadley, who faced a £35,000 disaster and the threat of financial ruin in the early days of setting up his galvanising firm, illustrates the

[21]

kind of resilience and resourcefulness small businessmen need in order to survive.

The near catastrophe occurred when some inferior zinc accidently found its way into his main galvanising bath, contaminating most of his stock. 'It stopped us dead,' recalled Meadley. The tank held 60 tons of zinc, which at that time cost around £500 a ton. Meadley still owed his suppliers around £30,000 and he was already two months behind with his payments.

The setback also meant that £1,500 a month would be added to the firm's gas bill, because it had to operate a back-up galvanising bath which was less fuel-efficient.

Most people would have thrown in the towel, but Meadley persevered and rode out the crisis, although it probably set his firm's development back by two years. One advantage he had was that before setting up his own company he had been a management consultant. He was accustomed to trouble-shooting, although the experience of going it alone taught him that there was a vast difference between theory and practice. 'I've become a lot more practical and down to earth since I started my own business,' he admitted.

One of the factors that helped Meadley piece his company back together again was the high degree of understanding shown by his creditors. It was as if they were willing him to survive. Both his suppliers and the institutions from which he had borrowed capital agreed to put back payments. Even the VAT men showed compassion and delayed demands for a couple of years.

Not all entrepreneurs meet with such sympathetic support. Malcolm Durrans ran into the sort of opposition that would test any entrepreneur's perseverance when he bought a small grocery shop at a picturesque fishing village. The shop was very cramped, so Durrans undertook alterations which tripled the amount of selling space. Other local retailers apparently saw this as a threat to their trade and they persuaded two manufacturers of fudge and toffee not to supply their products to Durrans.

His reaction was to set up his own fudge and toffee making company, which today produces tons of confectionery every week, which is sold widely in Britain and abroad. Durrans turned a setback into an industry worth hundreds of thousands of pounds a year, as well as providing badly needed jobs.

A less determined man might have given way to local pressure, but Durrans was made of sterner stuff. 'It depends whether you're made that way and whether you've already assessed what the profit potential of the product is,' he commented.

Durrans has the true grit that is indispensable to every small business entrepreneur. But that in itself is not enough. It takes a great deal more to transform the Would-be Entrepreneur into the Complete Entrepreneur.

Case Study A

Feathering his Nest

A mineralogist by training, Daniel Jaffe first became interested in feathers while doing research into new methods of pollution control at Nottingham University. That led to experiments in which feathers were used as a means to contain oil slicks.

At about that time, Jaffe was approached by a colonel in the Royal Scots Guards and asked to make an artificial feather mount for the regiment. The regimental plume up to that time was made from the feathers of the blackcock, a game bird that inhabits the Scottish Highlands, but which has greatly diminished in numbers in recent years. When the bird was declared a protected species the Royal Scots were left in a dilemma.

Jaffe's parents had once run a feather business for the hat trade, but he had never been involved in it. He nevertheless rose to the challenge and after experimenting with dyeing techniques, managed to produce a very passable imitation of the blackcock mount from goose feathers. The Ministry of Defence was so impressed with his handiwork that it placed orders for regimental plumes for other regiments.

The business blossomed and Jaffe went on to produce feathered bonnets for military and private bands in Canada, Australia and New Zealand as well as in the UK.

He soon learned that the secret of success in the regimental plume business was to dye the feathers in colours that withstood bad weather. The last thing a smart regiment wants is for the dye to start running in the first rainstorm.

Jaffe set up a dye works in a hundred-year-old grain store and carried out experiments to try to achieve the demanding specifications stipulated by the Ministry of Defence.

'Dyeing techniques are a long way from mineralogy, but having a scientific background certainly helped,' said Jaffe.

Jaffe had to become self-taught. 'I did it mostly by studying wool dyeing from books. But one of the biggest mistakes I made in the beginning was expecting to get the same sort of colouration with feathers as with wool. There are great similarities but there are specialised techniques for treating feathers.'

Once he had mastered the technique, Jaffe developed other sides to the business. He built up a good trade with florists, supplying dyed ostrich feathers for window displays. He also supplied coloured feathers for the fashion trade, particularly to leading milliners, including those who make hats for the royal family.

Seeking other ways to expand the business, Jaffe hit on the unusual idea of turning feathers into replica butterflies. He teamed up with an out-of-work teacher who specialised in textile design and screen printing and who became a partner in the business for a while. The delicate Red Admiral and Speckled Wood replicas that they designed together looked so authentic that the Natural Science Museum in London, the World Wild Life Fund and the British Butterfly Conservation Society all became customers. So too did Harrods.

Jaffe's company, with eight full-time workers and twenty outworkers, was soon turning out the delicate butterfly creations at the rate of 50,000 a year, helping to push his annual turnover towards the £250,000 mark.

The replicas had special appeal for the butterfly conservation society because it was felt that they could lead to a reduction in the number of real butterflies being killed to satisfy insatiable collectors.

Case Study B

Money in Magic

Like the sorcerer's apprentice, Edwin Hooper started something he is not at all sure how to stop. He began making tricks for magicians in a small room at his mother's home over thirty years ago and saw the business grow into the world's largest manufacturer of conjurer's equipment.

His firm, Supreme Magic, supplies conjurers and illusionists in practically every country of the world, including Russia. Leading magicians, such as Paul Daniels and the late Tommy Cooper, have been among his numerous customers.

To keep all these customers happy, Hooper has constantly had to invent new tricks and routines. He has built up a store of 20,000 different lines. When his expanding business became too big for one room, he took over a whole house. And when that could no longer contain the growth, he bought the house next door and knocked down the dividing wall. Then he had to build another store room in his back yard.

Even that began to overflow with spring-loaded rabbits, Chinese rings, guillotines, pop-flowers and all the paraphernalia of the magician's art. So he took over another sprawling set of premises, where row upon row of shelves became stacked with neatly packaged lines.

Keeping tabs on all the stock meant buying a £20,000 computer. 'Don't ask me how it works. It's a mystery to me,' revealed Hooper. Quite a confession from a man who has become a world authority on

[25]

the mysteries of magic and who once escaped from being buried alive in handcuffs.

To keep his hand in, Hooper attends a lot of magic conventions in this country and abroad. He uses the opportunities to promote his products and keep abreast of latest developments in magic circles. He prefers to demonstrate the ingenuity of his tricks rather than set them out on the conventional exhibition stand. 'If you do a demonstration you show the exact effect your tricks have on an audience,' he pointed out shrewdly.

Many of the products are his own inventions. Some of them involve money and he was once visited by American investigators who had heard that he was selling forgery kits capable of producing unlimited amounts of ten dollar bills. Hooper refused to reveal the secret of how the American currency was produced. He is adamant that once the mystery is taken out of magic by revealing to laymen how tricks are done, the bottom will fall out of the business. For this reason he only supplies his products direct to professionals.

His fame has become worldwide. He is the only living Englishman to hold the coveted Robert Houdini award for services to magic, presented to him by the French. He regularly receives bizarre inquiries from the strangest places. One customer wanted to know how the Indian rope trick was done. A customer in Africa asked how he could come by a love potion that had power over young virgins.

Producing all the tricks keeps a full-time staff of seventeen fully occupied and between thirty and forty outworkers are kept busy making such things as artificial flower bouquets.

Although his firm's success has become almost overwhelming, Hooper certainly doesn't regret the day he gave up working for a grocery firm many years ago to turn his passion for magic into a career.

He first got the magic bug at the age of ten when he saw the Great Levante performing on stage. Hooper gave his first performance at the age of fourteen for a charity show. For quite a few years, his hobby had to take second place to earning his living, first as a plumber's mate and then with a wholesale grocery firm, where he learned many of the operating principles he was later to apply to his business.

Eventually, however, he could not contain his enthusiasm for conjuring any longer. He went professional and specialised in children's parties. He got on to Harrod's books. The famous London store ran a theatrical agency in those days and young Edwin found himself in demand by some of the most important households in the land. But with the demise of the variety theatre and the general fall-off in live entertainment, Hooper found work increasingly hard to come by.

He decided to turn his experience of the performing art into a commercial venture. Most magic dealers at the time ran very limited operations, making tricks in small lots. Hooper set about building up a business on the grand scale — virtually applying the principles of mass production to what up to then had been largely a cottage industry.

He could not have envisaged what he was getting into. Slowing down the growth curve he then set in motion has proved to be one of the few tricks Hooper has been unable to master.

2

THE ONE-DIMENSIONAL ENTREPRENEUR

The Dangers of a Single Skill

FOR four years Gerry Tuffs seemed to be the very model of a successful small business entrepreneur. He appeared to be capable of no wrong as he set about building up a computer graphics company.

A former computer salesman, he planned the company's development in sensible, progressive stages. He began by servicing and repairing computers for educational establishments, which have a reputation for paying well and on time. With the profits generated from that piece of enterprise, he founded the company on a solid financial base. He then heard of an established American-based computer graphics company that was looking for an agent to market its products in Europe. Tuffs successfully applied for the agency, creating an important new strand to his business.

That too went well and soon Tuffs felt his company was ready to design and produce peripheral components for the American equipment to make it more suitable for the European market. The transition into manufacturing went smoothly and the company grew in stature.

By now, Tuffs' confidence knew no bounds. Everything he

touched seemed to turn to gold. There was no stopping him. The next logical step was to start manufacturing his own exclusive range of equipment. Encouraged by past successes, he was in no doubt that such a major step was within his company's capabilities. He reckoned the new products could be rolling off the assembly line within a year. He had no hesitation in budgeting for a doubling up of the £6 million annual turnover his company was already achieving.

But this was when Tuffs' run of good fortune came to an abrupt end. He had grossly under-estimated the task he had set himself and his research and development department. New product lines are notorious for running into problems. They rarely, if ever, materialise on time to meet production targets. Large companies, making a broad range of products, have the resources to ride out such teething problems, but Tuffs' company was still virtually a one-product enterprise.

Tuffs' budget calculations proved to be wildly optimistic and he had no real contingency plan to fall back on. To add to his problems, other aspects of the business were also beginning to go out of control.

When everything had been going well, Tuffs had decided to expand abroad. He hit on the idea of buying up failing companies in the United States and West Germany that were in product lines similar to those being produced by his own company. What he hadn't taken fully into account was that although he was able to acquire the sinking firms cheaply, he was also buying their problems.

It meant that half his time had to be spent travelling abroad on fire-fighting missions, just when he was badly needed at head office. It got to the point where he was torn agonisingly between dealing with the crisis at home and tackling the emergencies abroad.

Tuffs' carefully constructed growth plan began to crumble. The repercussions were extensive. When the company had been growing rapidly, financial institutions in the City were keen to share in Tuffs' success and to invest in a high-flyer. A regional development agency, too, was anxious to climb onto the bandwagon of success. It injected £750,000 into Tuffs' company, the largest single investment in a private company it had made up to that time.

But when Tuffs' appeared to be losing his golden touch, the investors began to panic. They put ever increasing pressure on him to get the company back on the rails. At first, Tuffs remained cool. He was convinced that it was only a temporary setback and that once his R&D department managed to get the new product range right, he would be able to get the company back on its upward climb.

But the delays in the design room grew longer and longer and the financial patching up Tuffs had to do became ever more desperate. In the end, to raise enough money to keep the company afloat, Tuffs was forced to dilute his own stake until he finally arrived at the point where he was no longer the majority shareholder. This inevitably left him highly vulnerable.

At the height of the crisis, he was summoned to a meeting of the institutional shareholders and was summarily dismissed. To his utter disbelief, the investors informed him that they no longer had any faith in his leadership and he was unceremoniously voted out of the company he had created.

Gerry Tuffs, who later went on to run another small computer company successfully, is a prime example of the one-dimensional entrepreneur. What he was good at he did superbly well. He was a super-salesman, a man who could win orders and convince financiers to invest in his ideas. But he was not a production specialist; otherwise, he would not have so disastrously miscalculated the time it takes to get a new range of equipment into production. Nor was he a financial expert; otherwise he would not have spread his resources so thinly or made such inadequate provisions for a rainy day. Nor was he a strategic planner; otherwise, he would not have steered his company into such a vulnerable position on so many different fronts.

His is perhaps an extreme case, but most small business start-ups are launched by one-dimensional entrepreneurs. They invariably start a company because they are particularly good at something. It may be, like Sir Clive Sinclair, they are brilliant inventors. They may be skilled at making things or at marketing or at juggling with figures. But however they excel in their single skill, it can never compensate for their inadequacies in the other disciplines.

No company can survive for long on a single outstanding ability. Sooner or later, the various weaknesses will outstrip the sole asset. Gerry Tuffs stayed the course longer than most. His vulnerability took longer to be exposed than is the case with many small businesses. Quite often the lack of all-round skills shows up in the early formative years of a start-up. The superbly-crafted products that were going to take the world by storm, surprisingly prove to have no market. Another entrepreneur's marketing skills might be wasted on a product or service that never stood a chance of having customer appeal.

Gerry Tuffs was a super-salesman who did not know enough about research and development. In one-dimensional small firms, the reverse can be equally devastating. The Pendar Robotics Group was formed by five engineers and scientists who had previously all worked in the same R&D department of an engineering company. After a long struggle for survival, the company finally collapsed with liabilities of over £2 million.

Bernard Capaldi, the company's charismatic executive director, largely attributed the downfall to lax management arising from the founders' one-dimensional skills. 'We had a relaxed attitude to management and would allow anybody to do whatever they liked,' he admitted.

The company started life as a trouble-shooting organisation, offering to solve firms' technical problems. But the founders gave themselves a free hand to pursue whatever product or service fascinated them as scientists without properly exploring whether the idea stood any change of producing satisfactory financial returns.

In particular, the company entered the highly precarious field of robotics before the British market was really ready to take it seriously. When the directors realised that this move had been premature, they attempted to retrieve a rapidly deteriorating situation by reverting to the original concept of solving specific technical problems for client firms. The switch in strategy came too late to save it from disaster, however.

It was perhaps understandable that a management team comprised entirely of scientists and engineers should allow their inventiveness to run away with them. Surprisingly, however, the group was backed by a syndicate of venture capitalists who apparently had not recognised the inherent danger in the situation. Five months prior to Pendar's collapse, the syndicate had injected almost £1 million in equity into the company.

This example goes to illustrate that however much money is pumped into a one-dimensional small firm, it is unlikely it will ever be able to overcome the lack of breadth in its management team. Indeed, the equity injection only served to aggravate Pendar's weakness and probably hastened its downfall. The £900,000 financial package cost the company about £130,000 in fees it could ill-afford.

There is probably no greater threat to the viability of a fledgling company than its one-dimensional creator. Yet it is an extremely difficult pitfall to avoid. It is a Catch 22 situation. In many cases, the small business entrepreneur will have hocked practically everything he owns to raise the necessary capital to launch his company. Hiring in professional managers with the relevant expertise to compensate for identified weaknesses will add to an already onerous financial burden and place an immediate strain on the firm's viability.

Turning to specialised consultants for help can also be exorbitantly expensive. The inclination of the one-dimensional entrepreneur is to bury his head in the sand, stop worrying about his weaknesses and concentrate on building up his company on the strengths he believes will carry the day. That often means enthusiastically turning out products for which he has no real evidence there will be a market.

To try to come to grips with the dilemma facing the one-dimensional entrepreneur, a whole plethora of advisory agencies have sprung up all over Britain. Some of them are government-backed, but quite a few are regional initiatives combining the resources of local government and the private sector. There are, for example, somewhere in the region of 300 enterprise agencies spread throughout the country offering free advice to small businesses. They normally have access to the kind of expertise that small firms lack.

Among a host of other organisations offering advice and aid is the Council for Small Industries in Rural Areas (CoSIRA), which helps to set up craft-based companies in areas of rural decline.

Some people believe that the proliferation of so many aid organisations results in a duplication of effort and confusion for those who could best benefit from the services. There have been demands for regional one-top agencies, such as those found in Scotland and Wales, to co-ordinate all the services, but so far the government has rejected the idea.

There is a powerful argument that local grass-roots agencies, serving a small community, is the best answer, but many of the existing agencies are under-funded and rely on the goodwill and hard work of one or two volunteers. Several of them face a struggle for survival similar to that encountered by the small firms they are supposed to be helping.

In any case, many business experts believe that such agencies can never really get to grips with the serious problems hampering the progress of the one-dimensional entrepreneur. They feel that such piece-meal efforts are only chipping away at a massive problem.

John Bradley is a former marketing director of Shell, and now serves as an adviser for the government's Small Firms Service. He is convinced that many entrepreneurs get into difficulties because they become obsessed with the brilliance of a new product and don't stop to think about the commercial implications of going into business.

He believes that all would-be small business entrepreneurs should attend comprehensive courses on how to set up a company before they even contemplate launching a commercial venture.

The aspiring entrepreneurs who seek Bradley's advice come from all walks of life – skilled tradesmen, professional people, inventors and engineers. 'The commercial aspects of turning an idea into profit is something which is almost beyond their comprehension,' he said, 'and they've wandered into difficulties unwittingly and are having to face problems which usually in the end convert into money problems, which they find insoluble. In fact, by the time they've asked to see us, we often find them insoluble as well, because they're so far gone.'

Bradley points out that although most of the difficulties entrepreneurs get themselves into can be diagnosed as marketing or financial problems, they in fact all derive from the same source – a lack of business training.

'The biggest problem of all is commercial ignorance,' he maintained. He insists that the Small Firms Service could be a lot more effective if would-be entrepreneurs were first put through short basic courses. One outcome of such courses could be that some people set on becoming entrepreneurs might well discover that they are not after all suited to the task, saving themselves much later heart-ache.

'Some people rush into running their own small business because they haven't been able to get on in big business or they may be unemployed and desperate,' said Bradley. 'Then you get the problem of commercial ignorance set against an overwhelming knowledge of how to make strip pine tables or whatever it may be. So you have got this total level of competence on the one hand and total ignorance on the other.'

Some of the larger enterprise agencies run courses for budding entrepreneurs along the lines Bradley is advocating. The London Enterprise Agency (LEntA), for example, runs linked week-end courses. Right at the outset it leaves participants in no doubt that they are going to be in for a tough time when they go it alone, that great demands are going to be made on their resilience and dedication.

Julian Sharples, director of a London-based company that creates jingles for radio and TV commercials, decided to attend the LEntA course because he felt he had been running his business 'by the seat of the pants'.

By the end of the course he had learned how to monitor the company's progress and adjust his plans to changing circumstances. 'Before, our book-keeper used to present us with the figures that told us how well or badly we had done in previous months. Our reaction was, so what?' he recalled.

Julian returned from the course so full of confidence about managing his company he at first became 'something of a fuehrer' to his staff of nine. But eventually he won their respect, because at last he knew how to run things professionally.

One improvement was that he and his two fellow directors, all in their twenties, defined their responsibilities more precisely. 'We used to go around tied with string, like three school kids holding hands. Every decision was a joint decision,' admitted Julian.

But possibly the most valuable lesson of all to come from the course for Julian was that he learned a lot about 'the psychology of the bank manager'. He was given the opportunity during the course to make a presentation to 'a real live bank manager', going through all the procedures of applying for a business loan. He found the exercise invaluable.

'How do you get to practise on a bank manager normally?' he asked. The experience has held him in good stead. The next time around it was the real thing. He soon afterwards had to ask his own bank manager for a loan to fund ambitious expansion plans.

But too often the lessons learned on training courses are soon forgotten and left unapplied once the over-worked entrepreneur becomes immersed again in running his company. To provide a more permanent watch on progress, some enterprise agencies, such as the East Devon Small Industries Group, have introduced 'Godfather' schemes. Small businesses that have approached an agency for assistance are put under the watchful eye of an experienced industrialist, banker or professional adviser, who visits them regularly to monitor progress and to ensure they haven't strayed too far from recognised business procedures.

The East Devon agency is one of the oldest in the country. It was set up by the local council originally to assist start-ups, but Albert Johnston, its development officer, found an equally urgent demand on his services from firms already in existence. Much of his time had to be devoted to firms that were in danger of being run aground by their one-dimensional owners.

'Small business entrepreneurs get so immersed in what they're producing, they tend to put financial control and administration to one side – until the crisis comes,' said Johnston.

Typical of the 'first-aid' work Johnston had to perform was that involving a small firm that came to him having run into a cash flow crisis after ten months of trading. The company's owners wanted to know where they could raise some money in the mistaken belief that this would solve their problems.

Johnston advised the firm that borrowing money without first tackling the root cause of the problem would only make matters worse. The company had no information about how it was faring and when Johnston analysed the accounts, he discovered it had made a £20,000 loss over a ten-month period. The company was also spending £12,000 in wages on two employees who were only producing about £3,000 worth of business.

Johnston helped the company prepare a business plan and a cash flow forecast. He then accompanied the owners on a visit to their bank manager, who was easily persuaded it was worthwhile providing the firm with financial assistance.

After another nine months of trading the company was showing a healthy profit of £2,900. 'It was quite a turnaround,' suggested Johnston. 'In another three months they would have gone under.'

The Welsh Developament Agency has taken the 'Godfather' idea a stage further. It has combined forces with the Confederation of British Industry (CBI) to introduce a scheme called ExSec, under which senior executives from some of the country's largest corporations are attached to fledgling small firms for periods of six months or more. Shell, BP, ICI and American-owned computer company Control Data are among the giant groups that have co-operated in the scheme by releasing some of their key managers for up to two years on full salary.

The small South Wales company of Air Space was one of the first to benefit from the scheme. When it came to creating giant inflatable play structures, Air Space reckoned it had the competition licked, but it soon discovered that it was not nearly so adept at structuring its own organisation.

'We were having a lot of trouble with inter-departmental

organisation, the way we work together,' recalled Rowan Watts, the firm's youthful managing director. 'We didn't have any real structure, so people were constantly, but unintentionally, going over each other's heads and behind each other's backs.'

Air Space was suffering from a problem common to most expanding companies. Its growth was outpacing its capacity to cope. The company's salvation came in the form of Evan Davies, who runs the ExSec service and also doubles up as one of its consultants. A congenial former senior manager with Allied Steel & Wire, a joint venture company between GKN and British Steel Corp., Davies has the quiet, unruffled nature that makes him ideal for sorting out the kind of turmoil that one-dimensional firms tend to get themselves into.

The one day a week Davies spent with Air Space was enough to get on top of the problems that were threatening its future.

Rowan Watts, a former photographer, with a flair for visual effects, and a partner who later left the firm, first got interested in inflatable play structures in 1979 while involved in a community project in Bristol.

They formed a company in 1981, working from borrowed premises in Bath. Unfortunately, they had barely got going when their main backer went into liquidation and they found themselves with a serious cash flow problem.

They approached the Welsh Development Agency, which saw enough potential in the company to justify a capital injection of £50,000 in return for a 29.9 per cent stake. This provided Air Space with the funds it needed to take off. It moved into a brand-new WDA factory and expanded its product range. In addition to the huge air beds, it was making inflatable advertising structures, such as a twenty-foot model of a sparking plug which Champion used to promote its products at Grand Prix races.

With a solid financial foundation, Air Space began to

expand almost as fast as one of its inflatables. Its turnover jumped from £8,000 in its first year of operation to £134,000. The rapid expansion inevitably put pressure on the company's structure and it was in serious danger of a blow-out. Davies went in with the brief of looking at how the company was operating from a stand-off viewpoint. In addition to the lack of a formal reporting structure, he detected weaknesses in the company's financial monitoring and concluded that its marketing was being neglected.

The company was failing to keep adequate records and was not following up many promising prospects. Davies helped Air Space to build up a bank of inquiries and institute a procedure for following them up regularly.

Davies also helped Air Space formalise some of its other vital procedures, including its costing systems. Previously, in making one-off inflatable structures for a particular customer, the cost of manufacture would sometimes exceed the quoted price, because the costing had not been properly carried out.

Davies was appointed to run ExSec after taking up early retirement from his previous company. More typically, ExSec's advisers are high-level managers on the point of promotion to more senior posts, but who could benefit from the broadening experience of two years with ExSec. The participating companies see the scheme as an opportunity for their managers to gain valuable experience. The executives are usually seconded to the service when they are about to move out of a specialised discipline into general management.

Big corporations, too, see the dangers of a one-dimensional outlook when their managers move into general management. In helping one-dimensional entrepreneurs, the senior executives are at the same time broadening their own horizons.

The participating firms are also motivated by feelings of

social responsibility. Control Data, for example, which claims to be the fourth largest computer firm in the world, with 60,000 employees globally, 6,000 of them in the UK, has always maintained a socially responsible stance and the Welsh scheme blends very neatly with the company's overall corporate policy.

ExSec has made no attempt, however, to match the skills of the secondees with the apparent weaknesses of the small firms it advises. 'It was felt it was better to get people who were experienced and who were holding reasonably senior appointments. The view was that with that kind of background, they ought to be capable of handling most of the kinds of situations that are likely to arise in small companies,' explained Davies.

The experience of most of the secondees has been that whilst their prime task in a small firm might have been to organise financial monitoring or set up a more formalised marketing system, one thing inevitably leads to another and they very quickly find themselves involved in all aspects of the business.

Observed Ken Charles, a senior financial executive with Control Data's Welsh subsidiary, who acted as a secondee for ExSec, 'If you are looking at the financial results, that automatically leads to general management decisions'.

Surprisingly few small companies make use of non-executive directors, one of the most effective ways of grafting expertise on to a one-dimensional business. A lot of entrepreneurs dismiss the idea because they are convinced that the non-executive director will merely add to the overhead burden of the company without contributing very much. They question whether someone who is only likely to turn up once or twice a month can learn enough about the business to be of any value.

This is a short-sighted view. A non-executive director can bring a broader perspective to a company and help an entrepeneur to be more aware of external factors impacting on his business. He can help with general strategy and help make contacts in areas of expertise that the small firm is lacking. It would cost far more than the £5,000 a year fees the non-executive director is likely to expect to receive if the entrepreneur had to seek such advice from specialised consultants.

The rise in the venture capital market is increasingly leaving small firms with little choice but to take a non-executive director on board. In many cases, venture capital firms make it a prerequisite before agreeing to invest any capital.

Colin Breed, a venture capital fund administrator, is a great believer in the benefits of nominating non-executive directors to watch over the fortunes of small firms. 'A non-executive director can take a more balanced view. He can provide new perspectives, helping the board to think through its underlying strategies and examine all its options.

'When we appoint someone we try to provide somebody who is complementary and also who can advise on the public presentation of the company. Big companies are becoming very much more aware of their public image, but small companies are less aware of what we call financial PR, the public perception. Small companies tend not to recognise the value of this sort of thing.'

Deloitte Haskins & Sells, a leading group of chartered accountants, has set up a panel of partners to offer their services as non-executive directors on company boards. John Finn, the group's senior management consultancy partner responsible for developing the panel, hopes that small firms will be among those taking advantage of the service.

'In our experience,' he said, 'small and growing businesses can benefit most from employing non-executive directors, because generally they have fewer management skills to draw on internally. The success of a business usually hinges on the management skills of the directors and often there is little margin for error in smaller enterprises. That's why financiers place so much emphasis on the people they invest in, rather than the products.'

There are many sources of help and advice the one-dimensional entrepreneur can turn to in order to compensate for his weaknesses. The important thing is for him to recognise that he needs such help. No entrepreneur can wear all the hats necessary to run a successful small business. Burying his head in the sand and refusing to recognise his inadequacies won't make them go away. In today's economic climate the small business entrepreneur needs all the support and advice he can find.

Trying to cope with a single skill is like trying to fight with both hands tied behind the back.

A recent study by the Business Management department of the Dorset Institute of Higher Education discovered that an alarming number of small firms are 'entrenched in the survival mentality'. In other words, it was evident that small businesses were so obsessed with seeking ways to survive that they devoted little or no attention to strategies for growth and expansion.

While many small businesses blame government red tape, employment legislation and excessive taxation for such narrow horizons, the real reason can often be traced to deficiencies in basic management disciplines. The fear is that if small business entrepreneurs expend all their energies on fighting for survival, they will never be in a position to make the contribution to the economy of tomorrow that everyone is expecting of them. They are supposed to be the wealth and job creators of the future. To achieve that goal, they need strategies that achieve more than merely keeping their businesses afloat.

The problem of the one-dimensional entrepreneur, therefore, is one that threatens not only the small businesses themselves, but the entire national economy and the hopes for future prosperity and job creation.

[43]

Case Study A

Robots Before Their Time

Bernard Capaldi and his four colleagues worked as a close-knit R&D team for a medium-sized engineering firm. They were very compatible. Then two of the team were made redundant. The five wanted to stay together and the answer seemed to be to go into business for themselves, selling their scientific skills to companies with technical problems.

At their former company they had performed trouble-shooting assignments for client firms and they took some of these customers with them when they set up their own operation. They also continued to work for their former firm on a contractual basis, using equipment for which the company no longer had any use.

'It was a fairly smooth transition,' recalled Capaldi, 'and I think the fact there was a team of us sharing the risk, the worry and the load made it a lot easier than the thought of having to do it all on one's own.'

In the early days, no clear leadership emerged, so the chairmanship of the company was rotated to give each of the five men experience of the top job. 'It worked for a while,' said Capaldi, 'and then you could see there were people floating to the top and those who really wanted to take different roles in the company.'

The five were reluctant to adopt titles because initially they worked together as a team of equals in much the same way as they had before, but it soon became clear that such informality could not last if the company was to be run successfully.

'I think the decision to give ourselves titles reflected the fact we wanted to get into business seriously,' said Capaldi. 'If you go into business, no matter what it is, you have to communicate with the outside world and the outside world expects to see certain things within a company – an MD, a chairman, a financial director and a chief engineer.'

The personalities of the five helped towards defining the different roles they should play. 'There were quiet ones and there were noisy ones,' said Capaldi, whose exuberant character clearly put him into

the latter category. 'There were those who were really only interested in science and those who were interested in overall administration.'

There was no escaping the fact, however, that all five directors had
a pronounced bias towards research and development that no
change of title could conceal. 'We were not businessmen,' admitted
Capaldi. 'We were engineers and scientists who were determined to
acquire a business capability, a commercial understanding and a
marketing understanding.'

They had no time during the hectic period of setting up the new
company to undertake any kind of business training, however. They
had to acquire their business skills as they went along. Day-to-day
experience had to be their learning ground. With hindsight, Capaldi
felt that if they had managed to attend a business and finance course
at the outset, events may have turned out very differently.

Their lack of a broad business experience led to mistakes right
from the beginning. Capaldi recalled with a shudder the company's
first appearance at a trade show when the exhibition stand they put
together without professional advice stood out like a sore thumb
among the more expertly prepared rival exhibits.

At first, the company sold its engineering skills to any customer it
could find. Eventually, however, it realised it needed to be more
selective in its choice of clients. It concentrated on what it regarded
as growth markets and made strenuous efforts to win over major
companies with household names. Once it had carried out assignments for companies like Rolls-Royce and British Aerospace, it was
not so difficult to convince smaller companies of its capabilities.

Eventually, however, the company's directors concluded that if
they were really going to make a go of it, they needed to get into
manufacturing. Robotics was an exciting field of activity with a
promising future. It appealed to their inventive talents.

They realised, however, that it was not an activity to be entered into
half-heartedly. 'It would have been a waste of time to build a robot in
a garage, selling it and hoping to build two more,' pointed out Capaldi.
'We had to do it in a realistic way and that meant shopping around for
a lot of finance.' The company managed to raise £500,000 in equity
capital as a result of a shares-and-loan package from a development
agency. That enabled it to go ahead with the prototype work on a
revolutionary, pneumatically-powered industrial robot, which sub-

stantially undercut the cost of similar machines on the market. This was followed by a more sophisticated, slightly more expensive robot.

Convinced that they were moving into a market with enormous potential, the directors lost no sleep over the large investment involved. Indeed, their enthusiasm won the support of a syndicate of venture capitalists, which poured a further £900,000 into the project.

Unfortunately, expectations were not matched by reality. Finding customers for the robots, particularly in Britain where industrialists were taking a very cautious approach to automation, was not as easy as they had surmised.

'People did not know as much about robotics as we thought they would,' explained Capaldi. 'We were selling robots in the wrong way – or more specifically we were marketing and selling ourselves in the wrong way. There was just no knowledge about the robotics industry. There was a lot of theory being written, but not many people were going around knocking on doors and finding out whether you could sell robots.'

A lack of orders forced the company to make a drastic switch in its strategy. Instead of promoting itself as a company that sold robots, it became a systems house, providing a complete turnkey service. It virtually returned to its original trouble-shooting role, offering to solve companies' automation problems, whether or not it involved robotics.

The company reasoned that if it helped to develop the automation market as a whole, this was bound eventually to stimulate a wider interest in robots. Unfortunately, the new approach came too late. The company's ambitions had outstripped its resources and it finally crashed with liabilities of over £2 million.

The company's plight was summed up by one of its financiers: 'Overall sales did not build up fast enough to cover costs. The robotics company was a lame duck before it became a systems company. But the change took time to become effective. Had steps been taken earlier, it might have been different. In future, we would want companies to take the systems route before we ploughed money into them.'

Capaldi too was left to ponder on what might have been: 'We should have been more single-minded. Money was wasted on interesting things, but which were not key to the company's activities.'

[46]

Case Study B

The One-Dimensional Locksmith

Jim Marten-Smith once owned a flourishing security firm, which, at its peak, was turning over £200,000 a year. But the firm outgrew his capacity to control it.

'It became a monster that was running me instead of me running it, because I found I hadn't got enough expertise around me,' he recalled.

In the end, Marten-Smith went into voluntary liquidation and shortly afterwards started up a more modest business as a locksmith. With an annual turnover of around £80,000, he had settled on a business he could control without the stresses and strains involved in running the larger operation.

A chartered accountant by training, he had taken on a variety of financial posts in companies ranging from agricultural development in Uganda to a meat firm and a gramophone company, before deciding to set up his own.

His final job was with a regional commercial television station. He was both company secretary and head of studio services, which encompassed an enormous range of duties, including labour relations.

'I found I was about 150 per cent committed. The job was a great strain,' he admitted. To add to the stress, he clashed with the TV station's colourful chairman. He was left no alternative but to resign and found himself on the streets without a job at forty-eight. He toured employment agencies, but soon became aware of an unpalatable fact of life.

'In 1977 there were very few jobs for chartered accountants and I was quite bluntly told I was getting a bit past it at my age. Most of the jobs had an age limit of thirty-five.'

The only solution seemed to be to set up his own business. Pondering on what would be the best field to set up in, he arrived at another inescapable conclusion. 'There were very few expanding sectors of the economy in 1977. There was North Sea Oil and there was crime.'

He couldn't see any way of breaking into the North Sea Oil market, but while he had worked for the television station he had got to know the man whose firm was contracted to provide the security guards. The two of them decided to start up a security firm to exploit the many opportunities they had detected. Marten-Smith put six months' redundancy money and some savings into the venture.

To ensure success, it was essential to make contact with the crime prevention department of the local police force. While doing so, Marten-Smith heard an off-hand remark about the need for more competition in the hardware side of security.

This prompted him to open a locksmith shop in a small side-street – a surprising decision perhaps for someone who had never had any experience of locksmithing in his life. Marten-Smith did not see that as a problem: 'I'd kicked around enough industries in my previous career to know that I could latch on to the bare bones of what made a business tick very quickly. I had been in warehousing, colonial development, the production of gramophone records and I had been in the meat industry and TV. You can't ask for greater diversity than that,' he suggested.

In fact, the locksmith business never really established itself, because it was tucked away in a small side street, hidden from public view. There were weeks when Marten-Smith did only £9 worth of business and he had to spend a considerable sum on advertising to make the service better known. The security guard side of the business took off dramatically, however, 'I swept the field on the security guard side,' said Marten-Smith proudly. 'I was very fortunate in the men I recruited. I succeeded in getting a bunch of blokes who were enthusiastic about being security guards. The net result was they always did their job well and the customers appreciated it.'

But as the business grew, so did the overheads and Marten-Smith built up a heavy VAT debt. In addition, he was beginning to find he could not control the many aspects of the business, for which he was responsible.

'I was perforce the best locksmith. I was the best expert in electronics. I was also the only person who knew how to run a set of books. There just weren't enough hours in the day to cope with all that as well as the odd emergency with the security guards.'

After the business went into liquidation Marten-Smith was approached by a firm that made burgular alarms. The firm offered to re-instate the locksmith shop in exchange for a sixty per cent stake in the venture. This time, however, the shop was sited in a more central location in the middle of a busy shopping area.

With this backing, Marten-Smith was able to build up a thriving business while keeping overheads low. 'I'm not making anywhere near the income I would have made if I had found a job as a chartered accountant. But I'm making a living, which is better than being on the dole,' said Marten-Smith, who had discovered that if you are a one-dimensional entrepreneur it is best not to set your sights too high.

3

THE HALFWAY-HOUSE ENTREPRENEUR

Safer Options: Franchising and Co-ops

WOULD-BE entrepreneurs who would like to start their own small firm, but who find going it alone a totally daunting prospect, can opt for alternatives that reduce the risks inherent in being a one-dimensional businessman.

One of the most popular ways of becoming a Halfway-House Entrepreneur is to take up a franchise. The franchisee enjoys the challenge of running his own operation, just like any other entrepreneur, but operates under the protective umbrella of an organisation with a proven concept. It could be said that franchising provides the best of all worlds – freedom of action with a degree of in-built security.

A survey conducted on behalf of the British Franchise Association (BFA) and the NatWest Bank revealed that there is a remarkably low failure rate among franchisees of around two per cent. The idea certainly seems to be catching on. At the last count there were around 300 franchise companies in Britain with total sales rapidly approaching the £2 billion mark, putting them on target to reach £5 billion in sales by 1990.

The survey among BFA's 100 member companies showed

that over 12,700 separate businesses are now operating in Britain under the franchise umbrella and that direct employment has reached 110,000.

The reason why so many first-time businessmen are opting for a franchise is that they are 'investing in a proven concept, because most franchises are established businesses', according to Christine Trueman, BFA's executive officer.

The range of franchises on offer has also broadened enormously in the past few years. Prospective franchisees now have a choice that spans small jobbing firms in carpet cleaning and mobile car tuning at the bottom end of the scale to major retailers and fast food restaurants at the top end. There is hardly any sector of commerce or the service industry that is not now covered by franchising. There is even a private detective firm operating through franchisees.

A major advantage is that banks are more likely to provide loans for a franchised operation than for unproven new start-ups. The reason is obvious. Franchises are already up and running and in most cases well established in the market place. Most clearing banks now offer specially tailored franchise packages and will usually provide up to seventy per cent of the required finance.

The banks themselves monitor the progress of the main franchise firms and in order to quality as a member of the BFA, a franchise company has to undergo stringent vetting. So anyone hoping to become a franchisee will be on pretty safe ground if he contacts the BFA first.

The cost of taking up a franchise varies enormously from around £10,000 for a small jobbing franchise up to around £350,000 for a major fast food franchise in London's Oxford Street, for example. In most cases the franchisee pays a once-only fee for use of the company's name (around £2,000 for a small operation) but he is also purchasing a whole range of back-up facilities, which can include stock and shop-fittings (in the case of a retail outlet), the benefits of national advertising, training and research and development.

But Christine Trueman of the BFA warns that franchising is not normally a way to make a fortune. Although one major fast food chain can probably boast a number of millionaires among its franchisees, this is very rare. A franchisee can normally only expect to start making a profit between eighteen months and four years, depending on the nature of the franchise.

'It's hard work; you've got to be self-motivated; and it can mean working long hours,' cautions Trueman. 'When a franchisee does fail it is often because he has become disillusioned from not making enough money soon enough.'

There are other sacrifices necessary in order to buy the comparative security of a franchise that may not come easy to the businessman with a true entrepreneurial spirit. The franchisee will have to sign an agreement with the franchisor that will restrict the former to doing things according to established practice. It will, for example, almost certainly restrain the franchisee from introducing new product lines from other sources or changing the shop's decor to suit his own tastes. The franchisor will insist that all products and services are obtained through him. The main aim of a franchise is to achieve unformity, so that customers are assured of receiving the same level and quality of service wherever they travel throughout the country.

The BFA advises potential franchisees to check out any legal agreement with a solicitor and to talk over the financial implications with an accountant. 'They ought to visit the franchise company and its offices to see the whole set-up and get a feel for it,' adds Trueman. 'They should have no hesitation in asking to see the company's accounts. They should get a list of the company's existing franchisees and ring a number of them at random and ask how they are getting on. The aspiring franchisee should make the choice about which one to contact, not the franchisor.'

The BFA receives around 10,000 inquiries a year from would-be franchisees. There are in fact more people waiting to become franchisees than there are opportunities available. So to win the franchisor's approval, the applicant needs to be convincing. There is little point, for example, someone with a shy and retiring nature applying for a franchise that requires a high level of selling power. But franchisors don't insist on any previous experience in a chosen field. In fact, they tend to prefer the applicant to be new to the field of operation. It means the franchisee will start with an open mind and is more likely to accept the franchisor's way of going about things.

Another alternative that attracts entrepreneurs who don't want to go the whole hog of becoming a lone entrepreneur is joining a co-operative. Because they are run by a group of equals, co-operatives have the advantage of providing safety in numbers. The combined talents of any group of people are always likely to outweigh the narrow abilities of the one-dimensional entrepreneur.

The popularity of co-operatives has grown phenomenally in recent years. Between 1970 and 1980 only 50 new co-operatives were registered in Britain, but since then around 1,000 more have sprung up. Like franchising, co-operatives seem to have the distinct advantage of a very low failure rate – in this case around six per cent.

It was this relatively high success rate that prompted the country's biggest and most enduring co-operative, the CRS, to launch a pioneering experiment in Cornwall. With financial backing from the Manpower Services Commission, CRS is helping unemployed people to start their own small co-operatives. It makes available expert advice, training, resources and rent-free premises. The initiative has given birth to ventures that include a horticultural business, a furniture recycling group, a printing co-operative and a building firm.

[54]

The experiment is being funded under the MSC's Community Programme, which aims to provide temporary work for the long-term unemployed. Managing agent for the Cornwall scheme is Jenni Thomson, who was attracted to the idea by the unusual survival rate among co-operatives. In looking for ways to alleviate the problems of chronic unemployment, Thompson was very anxious not to place already disillusioned people into high risk employment situations.

She believes there are some very sound reasons for co-operatives staying the course so well. 'I have a feeling it is the total commitment of its members, because they're not just committed to making a living; they're committed to each other, to the group. It's a shared operation and I think that sort of dedication is what's helping them to get through. Certainly, in the present economic climate small co-operatives seem to be the answer.'

The participants in the scheme attend courses at a CRS training centre, but CRS dispenses no financial aid. 'There's no point in giving people lots of money for them to lose it again. Co-operatives are not about the soft option and feather bedding. They're about self-reliance, but in a rather more sharing way than in an ordinary company,' explained Thompson.

The tentative entrepreneur who has serious doubts about his chances of succeeding in business might consider the option that probably calls for the least commitment – opening a market stall. This may seem a half-hearted approach, but it has the distinct advantage of testing entrepreneurial flair while keeping overheads to a bare minimum. One of the vital requirements of an entrepreneur is a skill to sell both himself and his products. A market stall soon shows up any deficiencies in these areas. A failure to succeed will dent the pride of the aspiring entrepreneur, but at least it will have made only a very small hole in his finances.

The London Enterprise Agency (LEntA) has compiled a

useful guide to running a market stall, which is appended to the end of this chapter.

Case Study

Co-op Gives Shoe Firm a Better Shine

When a major national shoe company closed down one of its regional factories, the chances of the 270 redundant workers finding alternative employment appeared remote. Sparse seasonal work at a local holiday camp seemed the only alternative to the dole queue.

However, from despair grew a collective spirit of survival which fostered the development of a co-operative at the factory. With the assistance of their former employer and their union, a core of employees banded together to get the machinery turning again and set the company on a new course in the highly competitive shoe manufacturing industry.

'We became like one happy family,' said one of the co-operative's four worker directors. 'An example of the spirit of the place was when we started and had no wages. Anyone who had extra lettuces or cabbages in their garden brought them in for the others.'

The establishment of the co-operative was first suggested during discussions between an action committee, formed to block the closure and the local Member of Parliament. The national shoe company seemed committed to closure, however, and a co-operative appeared the only realistic alternative to futile efforts by the action committee.

Apart from keeping their jobs, it offered the workers a chance to protect prized skills in the shoe-making business which could have vanished from the area for good.

'So many skills would have been thrown on the scrapheap,' pointed out one worker director. 'Skills are assets too and you like to think of them being handed down to the next generation.'

Of the 270 workers made redundant, about 140 expressed interest in the venture. However, restrictions on the co-operative's size during its formative stage meant that only 18 could participate initially. To avoid any accusation of favouritism, an independent interviewer was chosen to select the 18, according to required skills.

No bank could be enticed to back the venture, so the 18 were called upon to put up £500 each, most of which came from redundancy money they had been paid.

In the true tradition of a co-operative, all 18 members received the same pay. They all met once a week to discuss major decisions and the more menial tasks were shared out between them. By the end of the co-operative's first year of operation, a modest turnover of £50,000 had been achieved. But the road to success was a hard one. 'You can't imagine the heartbreaks we've had,' said one of the co-operative members. 'We were very green at running a business and we caught a cold one or two times. We didn't know anything about marketing.'

At first, before any volume of sales had been achieved, things looked very bleak. An appeal to the DHSS for unemployment benefit to tide them over was refused on the grounds that the co-operative members were continuing in their old employment – which they all felt was patently untrue. On top of that, the co-operative was faced with some bad debts that made its financial position increasingly vulnerable.

When it seemed that all was lost and some co-operative members were becoming desperate for money to pay their mortgages and support their families, rescue came from an unexpected quarter. Ironically, no sooner had the national shoe company closed down its factory than there was an upsurge in the shoe trade and it was experiencing difficulties in keeping pace with demand. It turned to the co-operative for assistance.

This gave the co-operative the boost in confidence it badly needed. Soon afterwards major orders came from other quarters. The co-operative eventually diversified its product range into bowling shoes, ladies sandals and leather handbags and purses.

The support the co-operative received from the national shoe company proved critical. There was still a year to go on the factory's lease when the co-operative was formed and the parent group handed it over for nothing along with machinery for manufacturing.

The essential ingredient for success, however, was the support the co-operative members gave each other and the strict adherence to the principles of egalitarianism. 'All we wanted to do was to be in employment, whether it be working for somebody else or for ourselves. We thought of ourselves as shoemakers not bosses,' observed one co-operative member.

A Guide to Running a Market Stall
(Source: London Enterprise Agency)

There is no standard procedure for running a market stall. The availability of space, costs, methods of hiring and restrictions on the type of goods which can be sold vary enormously.

It is almost impossible to start trading at a market without first becoming a 'casual' trader. Stands are usually hired out on a day-to-day basis by market supervisors on site. A first-come, first-served arrangement is normally operated, so queueing before daybreak is not uncommon and still may not guarantee a stand. At some markets, preference is given to regular casual traders.

There are usually long waiting lists for permanent pitches. When permanent spaces do become available, selection varies at each market. Some markets review licences annually; others operate leaseholds which can be very expensive.

Markets vary considerably, so it is advisable to visit the site first, preferably more than once on different days at different times to establish:

(a) the size of the market
(b) the variety of products on sale and whether certain products predominate on particular days
(c) how many stalls are selling the same type of goods as you, to compare prices and ranges

(d) by chatting to stand holders to establish opinions on the market, the amount of trade, the organisation, how long the traders have been using the market, how they feel about new traders
(e) how long the market has been running
(f) how popular the market is – if stands are too easily available it is probably not a very lucrative site

Some markets have specific days allocated to certain types of goods – i.e. food, antiques, crafts. If this is generally well known, it can create a captive audience for selling your products.

Check that your products are suitable for the market you have chosen. Some markets are renowned for providing bargains in certain product lines. There is little point, for example, in selling individually designed knitwear at a market where most of the stands are selling bric-à-brac or fruit and vegetables.

There are a number of clear advantages to running a market stall. They include:

1 A market stand can be run on a temporary basis, either for a few days each week or for a short period of time. This means:
   (a) a stand can be run as a part-time venture if you already have another job, or
   (b) act as an additional means of selling products you may be selling elsewhere.

2 If you are a 'casual' trader, the cost of running a market stand is low and normally without any commitment as to how many days you trade.

3 If a regular casual site or a permanent site is secured, a market stand can operate in a similar way to running a shop but with fewer overhead expenses.

4 A market stand is a means of conducting research into

your products if you have just started in business by:

(a) assessing the demand for your product

(b) the type of customer you attract

(c) an opportunity to talk directly to your customers to establish their opinions on your present products and find out their reactions to new lines.

5 Probably one of the best advantages of being a market trader is the enjoyment and personal satisfaction from dealing directly with your customers and meeting other traders in the busy, thriving atmosphere of a market place.

But while becoming a market trader can provide much of the excitment derived from being a fully-fledged entrepreneur, it is well to be aware of its disadvantages. It is very hard work, involving early morning starts, queueing in all weathers for a stand, suffering disappointments and wasted time if you are not allocated a space.

In addition, custom may fluctuate radically according to season and weather conditions. As a casual trader, at some markets, you may encounter some hostility from permanent traders who resent competition from people who trade at a market in addition to holding another job.

You should also remember that competition is likely to be strong from regular permanent stand holders who have built up a well-established trade.

4

THE IMPOVERISHED ENTREPRENEUR

Ways to Raise Capital

WHEN a revolutionary drill bit sharpener won two national innovation awards and then went on to take first prize in an international inventors' contest in Geneva, three would-be entrepreneurs seemed set to turn the idea into a money-spinning business. The invention the three men were pinning their hopes on operated as simply as a pencil sharpener and had all the hallmarks of a market winner. Indeed, a criterion used to judge the inventions in one of the innovation contests stipulated that they had to be ideas that could be turned into a viable business.

With the endorsement of so many experts, the three directors of Martek, the company set up to exploit the product, were convinced they would have investors queueing up to inject capital into the idea. They could not have been more wrong.

Their first approach was to a local bank to borrow capital under the government's guaranteed loan scheme. They had already sunk £20,000 of their own money into the project, mostly for marketing and tooling up. They estimated they needed a further £45,000 to get the company up and running.

They felt they had a pretty convincing case. Apart from all the awards, they produced a business plan that showed healthy profit projections.

The local bank manager referred the loan application to his regional office. The proposal was turned down on the grounds that although the figures looked promising, the project was too risky.

Undeterred, the directors decided to approach some City investors. By now, their revolutionary invention had caught the attention of several leading power tool manufacturers that were keen to buy the rights to it, but the directors were determined to form their own company and see the fruits of their inventiveness blossom into a flourishing business.

They were, however, prepared to give up a thirty per cent stake in their company in return for some equity capital, but they met with little enthusiasm from the City. 'If we'd been after £100,000 I've no doubt we would have got it,' said Gavin Carter, one of the three directors. As it was, the City turned up its nose at such an insignificant sum.

The next alternative was to seek the support of a local merchant bank, but the directors were told that its funds were tied up for that year. By now their spirits were beginning to flag, but they were advised to take their case to the Industrial and Commercial Finance Corporation, one of the country's leading investors in new ventures. Yet another rebuff. The directors were again told that the amount they wanted to raise was too little to be worth consideration. It was pointed out to them that it costs as much to administer and monitor a small investment as it does a large one. Therefore, small investments held little attraction for venture capitalists.

On the point of desperation, the directors outlined their plight to a local newspaper. The resulting article drew sympathy from a number of readers who decided to invest privately in Martek. Although each individual only had a small sum to offer, the total eventually amounted to £34,000, enough to launch the company. It had taken twelve months.

Soon afterwards, Martek introduced its drill bit sharpener at a major building trade exhibition in Birmingham and the orders came flooding in.

Although Martek appeared to be an attractive proposition for investors, it was probably lucky to have ever got off the ground. But for the persistence of its directors, it could still be languishing among the non-starters.

Starvation of capital, both to launch a company and, to a lesser extent, to fuel its growth once it is up and running, is one of the most serious problems facing the small business entrepreneur today. Bank managers tend to be a very conservative breed. Some would argue it is a function of their job to be that way. They are, after all, primarily guardians of their customers' wealth, which has been deposited at the bank for safe-keeping and in the fond hope that it will provide reasonable returns.

Few bank managers have themselves worked in a conventional company, let alone run one, so it is hardly surprising that they are more likely to offer backing to those who go along with tried and tested concepts, particularly as the demand for funds far outstrips the money available.

Someone planning to start up as a window cleaner is likely to receive a sympathetic hearing. It is something every bank manager is familiar with. It is not difficult to demonstrate that with a certain amount of industrious endeavour a favourable return on investment can be achieved. If, on the other hand, the bank manager is confronted with a new-fangled gadget, which the inventor insists is going to take the world by storm, where is the proof? How can the likely returns be calculated for a product the buying public hasn't yet set eyes on? Cash flow forecasts can only be an inspired guess at best.

Venture capitalists, on the other hand, expect to take risks. Many of them operate on the one-in-three formula. One project will go down the drain, another will tick over unspectacularly, but the third will be a shooting star that will make enough profits to wipe out the losses on the other two and make a tidy sum for the venture capitalist into the bargain.

But to achieve that goal the stakes have to be high. It is unlikely that a small firm, starting up on an initial investment of less that £50,000, is going to produce exciting returns in the short-term. It will take years for such a small operation to blossom into a major success story – if it ever happens. This unfortunate fact of life is one of the factors that has led to what has become known as the 'equity gap'. In the main, venture capital firms are reluctant to back projects that seek injections of less than £50,000. Some of the bigger ones draw the line as high as £200,000.

Where then are the small businesses – the acorns that are expected to grow into tomorrow's oak trees – to get their capital from? The sad fact is that there is very little start-up capital around, despite all the high-blown speeches by politicians and others about small businesses being the job creators of tomorrow. In the old days, start-up capital used to be provided by the proverbial Aunt Agatha, who invested her private nest-egg in a promising project dreamed up by a favourite nephew. Today, there is far less private capital available and what there is tends to be heavily taxed.

Start-up entrepreneurs are left with no alternative, therefore, than to borrow the money they need from financial institutions, seek equity or launch their companies on little more than a wing and a prayer, hoping that they will be able to finance the firm's growth from retained earnings.

With loans so hard to come by, many small businesses are started on totally inadequate financial resources. One estimate is that seven out of ten start-ups are launched on a very small bank loan or overdraft facility in the fond hope that the venture will be able to survive on retained profits. To some extent, this unsatisfactory situation was recognized by the government when it introduced the Enterprise Allowance

Scheme. It provides unemployed people wanting to start their own business £40 a week for a year with the idea that it will give them the opportunity to plough back whatever profits they make into their fledgling enterprises. The only financial prerequisite to qualify for the scheme is that the budding entrepreneur should have at least £1,000 in his or her bank account.

It is a source of great frustration to many small business entrepreneurs that they have such difficulty raising small amounts of capital to create new enterprises when there are vast sums of money circulating in the City of London. The terrible truth is that under existing economic rules, small businesses are not going to attract financial support on anything like the required scale when there are so many more appealing ways of obtaining returns on investment.

'It's been a problem for a number of years and I can't see any end to it,' laments Colin Breed, who administers a regional venture capital fund. 'It's all to do with risk and reward and the fact that ninety-nine per cent of all the venture capital funds are managed and controlled from London. The costs and risks involved are out of all proportion to the investments small businesses need.'

Breed sees little prospect of an improvement in the situation unless a way can be found to divert some of the huge funds being constantly recycled in the City into the small business market. 'The biggest institutions which have got money which should be directed into this field are undoubtedly the pension funds,' he declares, 'but there is no great incentive for them to divert even modest amounts of money into the small business sector. Who can dispute that putting their money into the Stock Exchange in readily marketable investments with the sort of returns they can get, is the best place? But it just produces a totally inflated stock market investment profile.

'Something like eighty-five per cent of all the shares on the

Stock Exchange are held by institutions. They have massive power and they're hiding behind this "duty of care" code to recycle the money around in the City. The amount that finds its way outside is miniscule.

'Even modest pension funds these days are probably increasing in value at the rate of £3 million to £5 million a week, simply from interest and dividends. That's an absolute nonsense. The money is being re-invested back into the old merry-go-round, while some poor entrepreneur in the regions is tearing his hair out to raise a few thousand pounds.

'Perhaps somebody ought to devise a way of encouraging the pension funds to place money in the bottom end of the market by giving some sort of tax advantage or by taxing the dividends at the other end.'

The government has made an attempt to alleviate the problem with the introduction of the Business Expansion Scheme (BES). Under this scheme, individual investors are encouraged to put sums of up to £40,000 into small unquoted trading companies in return for attractive tax relief. The money has to remain invested for at least five years. Otherwise the tax advantages are forfeited.

BES was launched in 1983 as a successor to the Business Start-up Scheme. It recognized the fact that private individuals were more likely to want to invest in expanding organizations than in start-ups. The scheme has undoubtedly generated millions of pounds that would not otherwise have been made available to the small business entrepreneur.

In the early stages, there was concern that a considerable part of the money raised was going into esoteric projects, such as art dealers and wine merchants, and into asset-backed organizations, such as hospitals and retirement homes, that did little to help the firms the scheme was supposed to help – those in the productive small business sector of the economy.

Adjustments were later made to the scheme to avoid these anomalies and there now seems to be growing evidence that small firms are becoming more aware of this source of funding and are making use of it in ever growing numbers. Some financial experts believe, however, that BES has already started to outlive its usefulness and that there is 'a degree of fatigue in the market'. A number of managed funds – the most popular source of BES equity – have already dropped out of the market, either disillusioned or because they feel they have squeezed as much juice out of the orange as they are likely to get. The prediction is that there will be less BES money around in future, adding to the problems arising from the dearth of funds available from other sources.

'There is a definite feeling that unless it is totally revamped BES is going to have problems generating sufficient interest in future,' declares one financial expert. 'It was set up without really understanding the market place. It was assumed there was some mechanism whereby Mr Smith, who had £40,000 to invest and would do so in a private company, actually knew that ABC company next door needed £40,000. Of course, no such mechanism ever existed.'

As a result, the administration of BES schemes gravitated to established institutions in the City, leading to increased costs involved in appraising and monitoring BES investment candidates. A survey conducted by the Small Business Research Trust two years after BES was launched revealed that the majority of the managed BES funds were operating from the South East and the Home Counties, once again leaving other regional small businesses out in the cold.

The Small Business Research Trust report suggested that one way to spread BES money into outlying regions would be to set up local investment groups like the US small business investment companies. It also advocated that investors should receive tax relief from the moment they injected their money into BES funds, rather than having to wait until their cash is invested in specific companies, as the current rules dictate.

[67]

This might help to reduce the disenchantment some BES investors are reported to be showing towards the scheme. BES investments are by their very nature risky. Otherwise there would have been no need to offer enticing tax incentives. But investors tend to forget the tax advantages and become alarmed when the companies they have invested in fail to show the returns they expected.

'I think there will be a lot of BES failures over the next couple of years,' predicts one financial pundit. 'Some will undoubtedly get to the end of their five year term and produce some reasonable rewards, but, like all venture capital, the lemons tend to ripen before the plums. Many people will suffer losses on their investments in the early years, which will make them think twice about putting more money into BES. They won't be prepared to take a balanced view and look at their gains and losses at the end of the five year term. Human nature being what it is, they will forget all about the tax refunds they have enjoyed.'

Despite such problems, the government undoubtedly regards BES as one of its success stories. It has been less happy with the Guaranteed Loan Scheme, which it also introduced to make more funds available to small businesses. The idea behind the scheme was that the pressure would be taken off both the banks and small business entrepreneurs by the government shouldering the majority of the risk involved in investments. Originally, the scheme enabled banks to make loans to small businessmen, eighty per cent of which would be guaranteed by the government. Disenchantment with the scheme grew, however, when it became apparent that the failure rate of participating companies was unreasonably high. The reason appeared to be that bank managers were ill-equipped to make judgements about the viability of business proposals and were invariably backing the wrong horse. There was also the suspicion that they were perhaps less thorough in vetting proposals in the safe knowledge that the government carried eighty per cent of the risk.

To stem the losses it was sustaining from the scheme, the government reduced the guarantee to seventy per cent and increased the premium. This simply had the effect of discouraging small businesses from considering the scheme because it had become prohibitively expensive. It also put a brake on the banks which were less inclined to risk catching a cold on investments in which they now had a larger stake. The whole exercise inevitably became self-defeating, since it meant that the impoverished small business entrepreneur was again being starved of funds he badly needed.

A strong rumour began to spread that the government was likely to abandon the scheme altogether, but instead it reinstated it in the 1986 Budget and reduced the premium again to make it less expensive.

In Colin Breed's view, the government's expectations of the Guaranteed Loan Scheme were too high in the first place. 'If the government ever thought it was going to make money on it in the short term it was deluding itself,' he contends. 'The idea should have been to try and create that seed corn of small businesses which would be the generator of employment in the medium-term. To think they wouldn't have to write off substantial amounts in the first few years was naive in the extreme.

'It's like most government – and even local government – initiatives. The expectations in relation to the resources committed are totally beyond what any person would reasonably expect.'

The Guaranteed Loan Scheme has a lot of critics, but some companies that have prospered on the strength of it swear by it. One such company is Hunter Electronics, a firm that buys electronic components from the US and sells them on to major UK manufacturers, mainly in the avionics business. Mike Ward, a former UK executive for the US-based group Motorola, who is managing director of Hunter Electronics, is convinced that the £75,000 loan he obtained under the scheme was 'exactly what we needed at exactly the time we needed it'.

He maintains that without the loan it would have taken many more years for Hunter Electronics to reach the substantial turnover it subsequently achieved. Ward set up the company in 1977 with a partner he later bought out. At first it traded modestly from a small 600 sq ft office. With low overheads, Ward and his partner managed to finance the start-up from their own resources. Their main business came from acting as distributors for General Semi-Conductors Industries Inc., an Arizona-based company that makes transient suppressors to protect avionics equipment from nuclear blasts and natural phenomena like lightning and static electricity.

But the distributorship represented a fairly narrow market for Hunter Electronics. In 1980, however, a major contract to distribute electronic connectors made by another US firm, called Robinson Nugent, came Ward's way.

In 1981, he signed a distributor agreement with the US company. But the key to making the operation a success was to buy in bulk at reduced rates in order to make Hunter Electronics competitive with the large number of suppliers already established in the market place. Ward needed to build a vast inventory so that he could react instantaneously to demand. He also needed to increase his workforce. It put the company in an entirely different league.

'Quite frankly, we had a tiger by the tail and it was quite clear that we were going to need a lot more cash to get this line going than we had hitherto anticipated,' recalled Ward. Up to that point, Midland Bank, recognizing the company's potential, had been 'very co-operative and generous' with the overdraft facilities it offered. Ward's predictions indicated, however, that he would need around £68,000 additional capital. He was realistic enough to see that his balance sheet could not support that kind of finance.

Ward rejected the idea of going for equity capital, because the amount of finance he needed represented more than a fifty per cent stake in the company. He also considered the idea of factoring his invoices, but concluded that it would cost him far too much. 'I could have hired a credit control manager for what it would have cost just to pay the standing charge on turnover,' Ward pointed out.

The Loan Guarantee Scheme seemed to be the only answer, although it certainly didn't come cheap. 'My attitude was that although the rate was penal in a way, it enabled us to buy in bulk and improve our margins,' explained Ward. 'This raises the whole question of whether the Loan Guarantee Scheme is right for small businesses. I believe it is suitable for some businesses, not for others.'

Ward borrowed the maximum amount – £75,000 – permitted under the scheme, with the government guaranteeing eighty per cent. He was offered the option of taking up a one year moratorium on repayments over the seven year term of the loan, but declined. 'I wanted to put a discipline on myself and make a go of it from day one,' said Ward.

As it turned out, he made the right decision. The strategy of buying in bulk from the US suppliers paid off so handsomely that eighteen months into the loan it was apparent Hunter Electronics could finance the business without it. Within two years it had paid it all back to Midland.

With the demand for capital far outstripping the available funds, it is the entrepreneur who presents his case clearly and concisely to the bank manager and who can back it up with credible cash flow forecasts who is most likely to win the day. It has been said that the first marketing test a would-be entrepreneur faces is selling himself to the bank manager. If he fails at that, he will probably never be successful in selling the products or services he intends to market.

There are a number of pitfalls entrepreneurs fall into when seeking a bank loan. The most obvious one is failing to do enough homework on the business plan before the initial interview with the bank manager. At one time, some of the blame for this could probably be placed at the door of the banks themselves. They made little attempt to spell out exactly what sort of preparation they expected a budding entrepreneur to make. The result often was that the aspiring businessman would arrive with a few scribbled notes on the back of an envelope.

He expected to win over the support of the bank manager by the sheer enthusiasm he radiated for his project. But bank managers are, if nothing else, pragmatic people who like to see evidence on which to base their decisions. It came as something of a surprise to the loan applicant when he was sent away to draw up a properly prepared business plan and to make the necessary financial calculations to support his thesis that he had a viable product idea.

Nowadays, banks take a lot more trouble to advertise the basic requirements for a successful loan application. All the major clearing banks produce a growing array of leaflets and booklets setting out what is needed. Some have even gone to the lengths of producing amusing videos which outline the pitfalls ill-prepared businessmen can fall into.

One of the requirements bank managers stress is commitment. They are likely to turn down requests from aspiring businessmen who expect the bank to carry all the risk. Indeed, it is very rare to obtain a business loan from a bank without being able to offer substantial collateral, often in the form of a second mortgage. It might be unfortunate that this sometimes precludes people who have a promising business idea with no assets of their own to back it, but the bank's view tends to be that the budding businessman is going to put a lot more effort into the venture if some of his own capital is riding on it.

Another misconception that many would-be entrepreneurs hold is the belief that one good idea represents a sound business proposition. Bank managers tend to look for a broader base and seek evidence that the single idea is likely to spawn a range of products that will ensure healthy future growth long after the original brainwave has outgrown its attractiveness to the buying public.

Bank managers are particularly wary of new inventions, which their inventors are convinced are going to take the world by storm, but for which it is almost impossible to produce any convincing market share projections. The inventor may be convinced he has come up with the next skate board craze, but bank managers are not gamblers by nature.

Aspiring businessman tend to be over-optimistic in their cash-flow forecasts. They usually start off with realistic calculations, but these often do not show the sort of returns in the early years that are likely to impress a bank manager. The temptation then is to inflate the figures to make the proposition look more promising. But bank managers are wise to such manipulations and will seriously question the business acumen of someone who resorts to such practices.

Often, small business entrepreneurs seek a bank loan when they might be better advised to opt for equity. There is a tendency to think only of the short term and not consider where the company should be heading in five years' time. When a longer term view is taken it often makes sense to consider equity.

'Loans are O.K. to begin with, providing you can service them within the general operation of the business,' points out Colin Breed. 'Equity becomes an essential consideration when a company expands beyond the retained profit capacity of the business. In other words, if it is not generating sufficient profit which it retains in its reserves to finance the ongoing needs of the turnover, it needs to obtain equity. The sooner it does it the better.

'Nine out of ten companies leave it too late. They can't bite the bullet early enough. The earlier you do it very often the better price you get and the more impact you can make later on. The later you leave it the worse price you get or you may not even get it offered at all. If you leave it too late, often the company is becoming stretched and its attractiveness is reduced. It's got high borrowings, tight cash-flow and large amounts tied up in preferential creditors. It almost becomes wipe-out finance.

'Whilst you are in a more relaxed situation you can demand a better price for your equity and you can use that money in a more cost-effective way. If you leave it too late, all you're going to do is redress the creditors' position, whereas if you bring it in early, you can use it to make capital investments for the expansion of the company.'

Normally, venture capitalists seek a twenty per cent to forty per cent equity stake in a company they are planning to invest in. They rarely ask for a majority stake because that is a certain way to kill off the motivation of the entrepreneurs running the company. On the other hand, they tend to consider anything less than twenty per cent as not worth their while. It also makes it difficult for them to have any real say in the company.

Increasingly sophisticated mechanisms are being devised now to gear the venture capitalists' stake to the performance of the company rather than settling on a fixed percentage at the outset. One fail-safe mechanism that is becoming increasingly popular allows the entrepreneur to win back shares from the venture capital investor when he meets or exceeds certain pre-defined business goals. This provides an incentive to the entrepreneur to make a success of his company and ensures a two-way bet for the venture capitalist.

Some venture capitalists offer a combination of equity and loans. If the company doesn't live up to its promise, the venture capitalist can cover his losses by obtaining repayments on the loan. If the company prospers, on the other hand, the venture capitalist reserves the right to convert the loan into equity and gain a slice of a growing business.

One of the problems of obtaining equity finance is the short-term view taken by City institutions. They tend to favour investments of two to three years' duration, whereas it is likely to be five to seven years before small businesses show returns that are attractive. As a result, venture capital organizations tend to spurn start-ups in favour of development capital situations, where the company is up and running, has a defined market place and strategy and is showing good potential for future growth.

A lot of small business entrepreneurs are reluctant to seek venture capital. They resent the idea of relinquishing a part of the ownership of the company they conceived and built up with toil and sweat to 'outsiders' who are merely contributing financial resources. A realistic way of looking at it, though, is that it is better to own say, seventy per cent of a successful company than 100 per cent of one that is about to go under because of lack of funds.

'Do you want a slice of fruit cake or all of a currant bun?' is the way Breed puts it. He argues that in any case talk of 'giving away' equity is totally misplaced. 'I don't know anybody who has given away equity. One in a hundred perhaps. All the rest has been bought for pound notes – often at a very high price.'

Although venture capitalists are more likely to back risky enterprises than banks or the more traditional lenders, they are nevertheless looking for winners and examine the prospects for success very closely before making an investment. Primarily, they are looking for firms that show signs of being well-managed and which have good prospects for growth.

Breed looks for what he calls the three Ms – Management, Marketing and Money. Is it the right management team to undertake the enterprise? Have they got a market place for the business they are going into? Is the financial package they are trying to put together, which may involve loans, equity, bank overdraft, factoring, leasing and HP, capable of supporting the business plan?

In the case of Martek, the financiers the company approached probably felt happy about the management team and the financial package it was attempting to put together. They may have had some doubts, however, about whether it had been established that there would be a market demand for the drill sharpener – doubts that proved unfounded once the company got off the ground.

One of the prime concerns of venture capitalists will always be the quality of the management of a company seeking equity. However much sense the business plan makes, the critical factor is the people who are going to implement it. There are basically two types of management that come under consideration – the one-man band and the management team, where a group of people with different disciplinary skills have joined forces to launch a new venture.

'Either situation can produce problems,' points out Breed. 'The one-man band certainly has limitations, because there's only so many hours in the day and if he brings in part-time accountants or marketing consultants, they won't have all their loyalties devoted to his company. But at least he will be keeping his costs down.

'If you go for a management team, to get the right people you often have to come up with attractive packages in terms of salaries or equity in the company, which can be quite expensive, and you don't know the team can necessarily work together. Just because you've brought the right disciplines together it doesn't mean they can actually work compatibly.'

To reach a conclusion about this, Breed looks at the track records of the people on the team, to make an assessment about what they are likely to bring to the new venture. He also looks into whether they have worked together previously for any length of time. Some venture capital firms will only inject funds into businesses run by proven management teams. For this reason, the lion's share of available funds is increasingly being invested in management buy-outs.

Breed also looks for commitment, which can take several guises. It can be apparent from a willingness to take low salaries while the new venture gets off the ground. Giving up a good job to join the firm is also an encouraging sign. 'I would be put off if the directors appeared to want to milk the company at an early stage,' says Breed.

When looking at the one-man band situation, Breed is definitely put off by 'the entrepreneur who insists he can do everything himself and is convinced he doesn't need any professional help'. A common problem is the entrepreneur who is obsessed by a new invention or by perfecting a device until the R&D costs outrun any prospect of being able to recoup them in the market place. 'That type of entrepreneur is very little use to us because his motivation is product superiority. The entrepreneur we like to see is the one whose motivation is unashamedly wanting to make money, because that's where we want our returns,' says Breed bluntly.

Sometimes requests for venture capital are turned down, not because there is anything inherently wrong with the proposal put up for scrutiny, but simply because the venture capital organization may have enough start-up companies on its books already. Every fund manager is anxious to establish a balanced portfolio that spreads the risks. However much they would like to support aspiring entrepreneurs, they cannot afford to have a portfolio that is overloaded with start-ups.

Venture capitalists are often maligned for taking a long time to make up their minds about a proposal. But Breed points out that the time is usually taken up by the entre-preneur in working out a viable business plan: 'What often happens is people don't get their act together quickly enough

[77]

and what could have been quite a decent little proposal then becomes very risky indeed because the cash flow has dried up, losses have accumulated while they've been inefficient or unable to sell their products and it then gets beyond redemption.'

Venture capital organizations often insist on nominating a non-executive director to the board as a condition of equity investment. The nominated board member is appointed to offer advice and monitor financial progress and the management of the firm generally. In some cases, the nominated director plays a more 'hands on' role in the company if the venture capital organization feels the firm has a serious weakness in the make-up of its management team. The nominated director will then be chosen from a discipline that complements the skills of the rest of the managers.

Once they have succeeded in raising the finance to set up their companies, many small business entrepreneurs neglect their ongoing requirement for liquidity. 'They often confuse profit with cash and the two are not in any way associated,' observes Breed. 'You can be extremely profitable, but short of cash. You've got to look after cash flow, because you can make a lot of money this year, but still be short of cash next year. Liquidity is an essential requirement for the ongoing development of the business.'

This is an area that can cause a lot of confusion among inexperienced small business entrepreneurs. They often boast that they are ploughing profits back into their companies and have no need of business loans. 'What they're actually doing,' points out Breed, 'is buying capital items out of revenue and decreasing their working capital, whereas they should be financing those fixed assets through long-term loans.'

Such misguided entrepreneurs eventually find themselves running out of cash. They haven't recognized that as their turnover increases so does their liquid requirement, basically to cover stock and debtors. Trying to support a growing turnover on an inadequate amount of working capital invariably leads to *overtrading*. The severity of the problem will depend on the kind of business the entrepreneur is running – whether he is in a cash trade or he is giving several months' credit to his customers.

'Overtrading really means you are taking on far too much business for the capital you've got to support it,' explains Breed. 'It becomes an inverted triangle. You have a very small capital base with a huge turnover. You only need one small problem or hiccup to knock the whole pyramid over. The idea is to try to increase the capital base on which to support an ever growing turnover. That's either done by retaining profits or by injecting outside capital or bringing in venture capital.'

One source of funds small businesses often overlook is their own customers. Many small firms apply for extra funding from banks or venture capitalists while they have large sums due to them from their customers. The problem is that larger companies are taking longer and longer to pay their debts. Small firms that are strapped for cash could often solve their cash flow problems overnight if they could get access to money owed to them more quickly.

The advantage to the larger companies of not paying their bills until they absolutely have to is obvious. At any given time, they will have vast sums owing to numerous suppliers. The longer they can keep that money in their bank accounts, the more interest they can earn on it, taking the pressure off their own cash flows.

As one financial observer puts it: 'No-one is going to thank a group treasurer for paying early when he could have had the money invested on the money market.'

The managing director of a chemical company acquired in a management buy-out discovered that the firm he inherited was several months behind in its payments to its small business suppliers. Morally, he felt compelled to redress the situation, but to do so would have cost him in the region of £750,000, which would have put the viability of his newly-acquired firm under threat. He was unable to do what his conscience dictated.

In such circumstances, of course, it becomes a vicious circle. Everybody is late paying everybody else. But it is the small business at the end of the line that suffers most – sometimes fatally.

Undeterred by the moral implications, the large companies play on the fact that the smaller firms cannot exist without their patronage and are therefore unlikely to do much about it. It is very difficult for a small firm desperate to get business to be aggressive towards the very providers of its livelihood.

The managing director of a small firm making industrial safety clothing found it almost impossible to be on the telephone seeking orders one moment and having to get through to the same company a few minutes later to complain about the overdue payment of bills. Psychologically he found the dual role draining. He would probably have become schizophrenic if he hadn't come up with an ideal solution. The answer was division of labour. His wife, who was helping him to run the business, chased the outstanding invoices while he concentrated on marketing.

But whoever has to do the chasing, late payments have become one of the biggest headaches for small businesses. The problem ties up an enormous amount of management time and puts a huge strain on the nerves of small business entrepreneurs who already have their hands full trying to run their companies successfully.

In one or two European countries the problem is regarded as such a serious impediment to the growth of small businesses that governments have brought in legislation that automatically slaps a penalty premium on companies that fail to pay up on time. Some observers feel that the problem will eventually have to be tackled by legal means in this country, but Britain has always prided itself on its ability to self-regulate and legislation is very much regarded as a last resort.

Increasingly, small firms are turning to factoring to solve the problem. This enables them to obtain up to seventy-five per cent of the value of an invoice immediately it is dispatched. The service doesn't come cheap and many small businesses see it as an extra financial burden they are unprepared to pay. Others, however, see it as a solution that is well worth the price.

Factoring does far more than improve a small firm's liquidity. It can smooth a firm's cash flow and help it forecast financial progress more accurately. It can do away with the necessity for a sales ledger and credit control team, thus saving on the wages' bill. It also provides an in-built insurance for bad debts and for exporting firms it reduces the hassle involved in collecting debts from overseas customers.

The evidence is that an increasing number of small firms are seeing the good sense of adopting factoring as a means to reduce the pressures on cash. In 1985, the UK's eight largest factoring companies – which form the Association of British Factors – handled over £4.6 billion worth of business, up twenty per cent on the previous year. Over half of their clients had a turnover of less than £500,000.

When the two directors of a sportswear business achieved a breakthrough by obtaining the major order they had always dreamed of from a leading mail order firm, they were immediately faced with the problem of how to finance the deal. The order for 23,000 swimsuits was far larger than anything they had handled before and they badly needed additional finance to pay for new machinery and materials.

Their solution was to opt for the NatWest credit factoring scheme, which guaranteed them seventy per cent of the value of the invoices on dispatch. The service didn't come cheap at an initial charge of 1.5 per cent of sales, but the directors saw it as their only means of survival in business. 'It took all the worry out of it,' said one director. 'We didn't really have much choice. We couldn't have got the money any other way.'

Some experts argue that factoring should simply be regarded as another form of borrowing. Observes Breed: 'It's a help because it cuts out the waiting time, but you pay heavily for that and it never improves the gearing of the company, because it actually increases the borrowing.

'The banks have utilized factoring as a means of getting more profit out of their organizations, because whereas banks used to provide certain cover for debtors under a floating charge, their degree of control over the debtors and the sales ledger was virtually non-existent. Factoring organizations, often subsidiaries of the major clearing banks, actually take over the ledger. They are much more able to monitor closely a company's debtor profile and lend against it than the traditional clearing bank operation.

'The good point about factoring is that it tends to increase as the business expands, so that it is a percentage of the overall debtors. Whereas you would be continually having to go back to the bank and ask for an increased overdraft to cover your working capital requirements, this automatically grows with you. Another advantage is that factoring companies often keep black lists. While a big company might decide not to pay a small company at the due date, it might think twice when it involves a factoring company which might decrease the big company's credit rating.'

Not everyone believes it is necessary to resort to factoring to control the bad debts problem, however. Some experts believe a lot can be achieved by more efficient credit control. 'The name of the game is not debt collection; it's cash flow,' suggests one expert. 'What many small companies fail to realize is that debtors are the easiest form of finance they can put their hands on.'

Instead of looking at the issue in this way, most small firms behave like bad bankers. They lend money to their customers through selling goods and services on credit. They earn no interest on what they have lent. They don't seem to grasp the point that sales are not really sales until the customer has actually paid. The transaction remains a free loan while the cash is outstanding. Big companies regard living off such free loans as fair game in business life.

A lot of the blame rests with the small business entrepreneurs themselves. Many of them do not bother to set up efficient systems for keeping on top of outstanding debts. (See appendix at the end of this chapter.)

A growing number of companies that manage to overcome the problems of growth and raising finance eventually aspire to a flotation on the Unlisted Securities Market (USM). Going public provides the opportunity to market a company's shares to raise capital and for other shareholders to obtain a return on their investment.

The USM was established in 1980 as a second-tier securities market for small- to medium-sized firms which for one reason or another were unable or did not wish to obtain a full listing on the Stock Exchange. The requirements for a USM listing are far less stringent than those for a full listing. The average cost of a flotation at around £170,000 is considerably cheaper than a full listing. In addition, a company can qualify for the USM without having to release more than ten per cent of its shares, whereas twenty-five per cent of a company's equity has to be in the hands of the public to achieve a full Stock Market listing.

To justify the cost of a USM flotation, a company probably needs to have a turnover of between £5 million and £7 million and pre-tax profits of around £500,000, though companies with lower turnovers have found their way on to the market. The success of the USM has exceeded most expectations. In the first five years, around 400 companies joined it and £1 billion was raised. It turned numerous small business entrepreneurs into millionaires and there have been very few failures to date.

It has been so successful, in fact, that there have been few transfers from the USM to the upper house of the Stock Market. Few USM companies have seen any point in incurring the considerable costs of going for a full listing.

A third tier was recently added to the Stock Market specifically aimed at better regulation of the issue and trading of shares in small companies. Entry into the Third Market, as it is known, is far less restrictive than the rules governing membership of the two higher tiers. There is no restriction on size or age for companies wishing to join the Third Market.

According to the rules, a company must have audited accounts for at least one full year to qualify, but exceptions may be made in cases where companies can show they have fully researched and costed a project. In theory, 'green field' companies can participate, which could provide a valuable new way for struggling start-ups to gain access to badly needed capital.

One City expert welcomed the addition of the Third Market as 'a great opportunity for private individuals to invest in venture capital and management buy-out situations which have hitherto been the province of the institutions'.

There are two other methods of going public. One is via the Over the Counter (OTC) market. This market has been created by licensed dealers to enable public trading to take place in securities outside the Stock Exchange. The OTC is widely regarded as a high risk/high reward market. It is also somewhat narrow and not normally used for large fund-raising exercises. Some companies see the OTC as giving greater security against unwanted takeover bids, even though a lower price earnings ratio may result.

A fourth market is available in the form of a private placing of shares with investors introduced by professional advisers. An increasing number of investors are showing interest in this market, an interest that has been accentuated with the introduction of BES. But it still represents a very small part of the total market. Very few companies obtain funding from private placings.

The USM, too, for all its glamour and reputation for creating millionaries, is only nibbling at the vast problem small businesses in Britain face in raising capital to fuel their growth. Financial pundits are pessimistic that unless some major new measures are introduced to channel large capital resources into the small business sector, the impoverished entrepreneur cannot expect things to get any better. In a free market, finance gravitates to those areas of the economy where quick returns can be earned from copper-plate investments.

Small businesses can never offer instant rich pickings. They have difficult births and they cannot be expected to become profitable overnight. In such circumstances, Britain's small businesses will continue to live in a financial jungle where the principal rule of the game is the survival of the fittest.

Case Study A

The End of a Revolution

When Whyteleafe Scientific Ltd., a firm making high-tech laboratory equipment, went into liquidation in 1984, a leading accountancy group brought in to investigate the firm's collapse, attributed it to several shortcomings common to struggling new ventures.

They included under-capitalization, poor financial management control of the company's resources, inadequate monitoring of development and production costs, and lack of turnover due to weak marketing.

The company had been set up by Dr Martin Pickard to market a new type of laboratory centrifuge with which he hoped to advance the frontiers of scientific research. The centrifuges rotated laboratory samples at speeds of up to 12,000 revs per minute. At that rate of revolution a G-force equivalent to several tons is generated causing solids to separate from liquids in a matter of seconds.

The technique is widely used in medical research to separate red blood cells from plasma, for example. Other samples commonly subjected to this treatment include urine, liver samples and brain samples.

Said Dr Pickard: 'Nearly all biological processes that occur in research laboratories have a separation procedure as a first step. You'd be hard put to find a biological laboratory without a centrifuge of some sort in it.' So the market potential of a revolutionary new centrifuge system developed at Whyteleafe seemed enormous.

One of the instrument's main areas of application was in the intriguing field of biotechnology, which involves genetic engineering. Centrifuges of a similar type that were already on the market were selling at around £40,000. Dr Pickard predicted that his machine which would be more compact than existing models, would sell at around £10,000, opening up a 'terrific international market'.

Before setting up his own business, Dr Pickard had carried out biochemistry research at Nottingham University's medical school. 'Pure research after ten years gets very tedious,' he said. 'There's no longer any more challenge. I had my research mapped out for the next twenty to thirty years. I could tell you exactly what I was going to do – even when the breakthroughs were going to come within a year or two.'

So Dr Pickard left what he described as 'the closeted academic world' and joined a scientific equipment firm – a subsidiary of Fisons. But that only served to convince him that he didn't want to work for a large group. 'I am primarily an ideas man and an innovator. I came up against an enormous inertia to new ideas,' he recalled.

So with very limited financial resources he formed Whyteleafe in May 1981 together with a metallurgical expert he had been working with at the Fisons' subsidiary. A good understanding of how metals would react to the stresses generated by such high G-forces by the centrifuges was vital to the venture's success. Special alloys and casting techniques were necessary to produce a machine that could stand up to the strain. The casting was done by a London firm which also made the castings for Formula One racing cars.

It took the two men about six months to go into production with a prototype, working with a couple of lathes and a milling machine in a small back garden shed. They eventually expanded into a 400 sq ft prefabricated garage. When they outgrew this they looked around for proper workshop facilities and eventually moved into a small unit on a new industrial estate.

By the second year of trading, they had built up to a turnover of £70,000, but costs were rapidly outstripping income. It soon became clear that a bold venture that had set out to challenge the major manufacturers of medical equipment had run out of financial steam and would have to go into liquidation.

Case Study B

Credit Factoring to the Rescue

When Coats Paton closed down one of its sportswear subsidiaries, two of the firm's employees made up their minds to go into business to prove such an operation could be made viable.

The two men who decided to go it alone were Keith Quinn, formerly a salesman for the subsidiary firm and Terry Chynoweth, who became financial director of the new venture. The company they set up – South West Leisure Products – grew so fast that the two entrepreneurs experienced difficulty in raising enough finance to fund the expansion. It was only by keeping overheads low and by generating extra cash through the NatWest credit factoring scheme that the company was prevented from getting out of control.

Credit factoring provided the company with the opportunity to obtain from NatWest seventy per cent of the value of invoices on dispatch, creating badly needed capital to pay for machinery and materials for some of the huge orders it had been winning from such prestigious organizations as British Mail Order Catalogue, Debenhams and Slazenger.

The quality of its sportswear became so highly prized that it was selected to supply track suits for the World Water Ski Championships and skating dresses for the World Roller Skating Championships.

The track suits had to be individually embroidered with the flags of seventeen competing nations. The firm decided to buy a new automated embroidery machine to tackle such intricate work.

It didn't take Quinn long to realize that his private garage would be inadequate to contain the rapid growth of his fledgling firm, which he set up with the help of a fixed-interest business development loan of £5,000 from NatWest. Before long the company had moved into several units on an industrial estate taking up a total of 1,500 sq ft.

For a year, Chynoweth stayed on as company secretary for another company to avoid draining the resources of South West Leisure Products by drawing a salary. He helped Quinn build up the business in his spare time until the company was sufficiently well-established for him to join it full time.

As the company expanded rapidly, NatWest agreed to increase the business loan to £10,000, secured against the houses of the two directors and provided a £5,000 overdraft facility. Even this was insufficient to fuel the growth. So the firm obtained an additional £25,000 equity infusion from a local enterprise fund.

The two directors admitted that luck was on their side in making such rapid progress. Without it, it could well have been a very different story. 'We were in the right place at the right time,' said Chynoweth. 'We came into the business just as the government was putting quotas on imports from Taiwan. A lot of companies had to look for new suppliers in the UK. We seized the opportunity.'

The real breakthrough came when they won an order for 23,000 swimsuits from British Mail Order Catalogue. Quinn had approached them originally with the firm's line of leotards, but because of start-up problems he was too late for the next season's selection. A few weeks later, however, BMOC, hit by the government quota on imports, came back to South West Leisure Products and asked it to make swimsuits to an established design – known as copy-make in the trade.

'The first order was worth £6,000,' recalled Quinn. 'We worked like blazes to get that one out on time. Then we got a follow-up order and a final order which pushed it up to around 23,000 garments.'

The success of this exercise convinced Quinn and Chynoweth that swimwear had a greater market potential than leotards. The firm went on to produce four different styles of swimwear, designed by Quinn's wife, Sheena. The two directors knew the swimwear market in Britain was huge. One company alone was producing 30,000 suits a week. They were convinced they could beat most of the competition for price and could equal their quality. But to be truly competitive, they had to develop their own brand-name products.

Funding such rapid expansion was a continual drain on the firm's financial resources. By the time it was approaching a turnover of £1 million, Chynoweth saw the need to consolidate. 'We really need to get some money behind us,' noted Chynoweth. 'The only way is to retain our profits. Up to now all the profits we've made have gone into machines and stocks. We've generated assets rather than cash.'

During this expansionary phase, credit factoring was the financial life-line that kept the company going. At an initial charge of 1.5 per cent of sales, the service didn't come cheap. 'But it took the worry out of it,' observed Chynoweth. 'We didn't really have much choice. You can't get the money by any other means.'

A Guide to Proper Credit Control

Any company that fails to set up a proper credit control system can end up going out of business because of an inability to collect money genuinely due to it. There are a number of well-established guidelines for avoiding bad debts:

- Establish a systematic procedure. Where possible, send invoices out on the same day as the goods or services provided
- Ensure that invoices are properly prepared; that they

carry an order number and bear the name of the person who normally deals with them

- Check that invoices and correspondence are properly addressed
- Make sure that customers understand the terms and conditions of payment at the time the order is discussed. Remember to state them clearly on all necessary documents.
- Challenge any terms of payment you consider unfair and liable to harm your business – 'No payment for ninety days', for example. Be sure you know what you are letting yourself in for
- Develop a proper collecting procedure. Send out statements on time, for example
- Don't be afraid to ask for the money once it becomes due. Don't let an old debt become a bad debt.

It might also be a good idea to offer a settlement discount for early payment or to charge interest for every month payment is overdue. But both should be made clear in the terms of payment. Administering such schemes, however, can sometimes give more problems than they solve.

Small firms that rely on one or two major companies for their income are particularly vulnerable to the problem of bad debts. One solution is to bring the big companies out of their environment and down to your level. With a little research it should not be difficult to find out the name of the financial director of a guilty big company. Telephone him at home, apologise for the disturbance, but explain how vital prompt payment is for the survival of your business.

If you are supplying him with good quality products, it will not be in his interest for you to go out of business, but, more importantly, he will not wish to be contacted at home again and will probably make every endeavour to ensure you are paid on time in future.

5

THE BLINKERED ENTREPRENEUR

Getting the Marketing Right

ONE summer, Gwyn Lawrence decided he would go into business to make the perfect sundial. He was convinced that by combining sixteenth century craftsmanship with modern-day computer technology, he could produce a sundial that was fastidiously accurate, aesthetically appealing and that would last for 500 years.

Two years later when he had come close to achieving his aim, Lawrence seriously questioned whether it had all been worth the effort. He had sold his house, his car and his stereo equipment to finance two years' research into the project. The end result was an exquisite sundial, but he was left in considerable doubt about whether perfection was a commercially viable proposition.

Lawrence epitomizes the one-dimensional entrepreneur who believes that all he needs to do is to come up with an outstanding product and everything else will take care of itself. He went to infinite trouble to research what needs to go into the perfect sundial, but he did precious little *market* research to find out whether in fact there was anybody who wished to buy such an expensive product.

There is a misconception among inexperienced entrepreneurs that good ideas sell themselves. Come up with a
novel product line and the customers will automatically beat
a path to your door. The market place is strewn with ruined
businesses that take such a naive view.

Lawrence realized his error in sufficient time to moderate
his idealism. From the costly experience of researching and
producing his perfect sundial, he eventually learned the
lesson that the public is more likely to want less than perfection at a price it can afford. By adjusting his designs, Lawrence produced a range of less ambitious sundials that
enabled him to run a viable business.

Consultant Ian Jennings defines marketing as 'the process
which makes profitable sales inevitable'. Too often, he
observes, marketing is confused with advertising.

'Many businesses are founded because the principals
know how to make something which their instinct tells them
someone else wants, although it rarely tells them how many,
when or at what price. This is where marketing should begin
and instinct end,' he suggests.

To ascertain whether a product idea is likely to appeal to
sufficient customers to justify turning it into a business takes
a good deal of market research. Oddly enough, most aspiring
entrepreneurs spend more time exploring the market for a
new car than they do researching the market place for a new
product idea.

Many of them are reluctant to call on the help of marketing
consultants in the belief that they will produce heavy tomes
written in jargon it will be impossible to comprehend.

Ian Griffith, marketing director of the Institute of
Marketing, points out, however, that there is a lot of basic
market research that the start-up entrepreneur can conduct
for himself. All he will need to invest is his time and a certain
amount of foot-slogging.

By simply calling at his local library, the would-be entrepreneur can leaf through trade magazines that are full of statistics about various market sectors. There are also government reports that give useful statistics about market shares.

'What we say pretty strongly is that before you actually start to invest time and money creating a product which you believe in, you must first try to find out something about the market place it will live in and who it might appeal to,' says Griffith.

'If you're offering a product that is going to be sold through a retail outlet, take a walk down your local high street and look around you. Look at the outlets that are selling similar sets of products. Look at how they're selling, what they're priced at, how they are presented. Try and get some idea of how the distributive trade actually works.

'You may even discover that what you thought was a unique product idea has already been thought of by somebody else.'

Such a discovery wouldn't do a lot for the morale of the would-be entrepreneur, but it might prevent him from investing his life's savings in a product idea that was doomed to failure.

The simple truth is the more you find out about your potential market in advance the less likely you are to be taken by surprise. When Joanna Sheen decided to start up her business selling pictures made from pressed flowers, her husband, Adrian, went out selling some of the early samples at local markets. He also set up stands at dozens of agricultural shows to display the pictures and get feedback from the general public. He regarded the experience as invaluable.

'From selling direct to the public you learn an awful lot about whether your products will sell in the first place and secondly what price they can realistically sell at,' says Adrian Sheen.

Once Pauline Ralph had made the first prototype of the

thatched cottage musical boxes she hoped to turn into a viable business, her first attempt to sound out the market place was a tour of local souvenir shops. To her surprise, this basic exercise in market research yielded dividends beyond her wildest hopes. She returned home, exhilarated and bemused, with an order for six dozen musical boxes.

'I rang my husband Ken in a panic,' she recalled with amusement. 'I hadn't any idea how I was going to make so many. I wasn't even sure I should accept the orders. Ken advised me to go ahead, saying we could work out how we were going to make them afterwards.'

The next week-end the couple went into action, while their children took over the household chores. By the early hours of Monday morning they had glued together three dozen little thatched cottages, which they left to dry in the spare room.

'The next day I went into the room to look at them and every single one had warped. We'd used the wrong kind of wood. It was dreadful,' recalled Pauline.

The Ralphs had perhaps jumped the gun in translating their market research into action before they had set up proper production facilities, but that was a problem they could soon put right. They hired the assistance of an experienced carpenter, who soon advised them what they were doing wrong. A more disastrous outcome could have resulted if the Ralphs had gone into production before testing the reaction of the market place to their ideas.

One of the decisions the start-up entrepreneur has to make sooner or later is whether to go for a mass market or try to produce a specialized product or service. On the face of it, mass markets seem to be more attractive. The more potential customers the better. But marketing experts point out that the bigger the market, the bigger the competition. Finding the right market niche for a specialized product might be more difficult initially, but once it has been identified, the would-be entrepreneur could find that he has it pretty much to himself.

[94]

The aspiring entrepreneur should never be vague about the market he is going after. The ones that succeed usually know very precisely the narrow segment of the market they intend to attack.

When Monty Don and his partner, Sarah Erskine, decided to go into the jewellery designing business, they spurned the lure of mass markets and concentrated on producing jewellery tailor-made for leading fashion houses. They firmly believed that jewellery should be designed to complement fashion rather than being added as an after-thought.

To their surprise, the couple discovered that this was such a novel approach that they virtually had the market to themselves. Their jewellery has since become highly sought-after by famous fashion houses and by film and TV producers.

'Very quickly – within eighteen months of setting up – we were the best selling jewellery designers in London,' says Monty Don, a Cambridge graduate. 'But the truth is we had no competition. It was a big open door and we just walked through it. Until we came along, fashion designers had to take whatever jewellery was going from the wholesalers.'

The couple started with very little capital and spent most of it on sales promotion. They ordered expensive colour pictures of their original designs, which they sent to 'every magazine in the country and every London newspaper'. They followed this up with a visit to the publications, Monty charming his way into the offices of fashion editors.

'If he wasn't getting any attention, he would drape the office typist in a tiara and make everyone look at her,' recalled Sarah. It proved highly effective, as several weighty scrap books containing press cuttings can testify.

They then made a grand tour of leading fashion houses to convince them that jewellery should be an integral part of their fashion designs. It took awhile for the fashion houses, nervous about revealing their latest designs, to take Monty and Sarah into their confidence. But eventually one of the fashion houses gave them a chance to design jewellery for an important collection.

'We borrowed £2,000 from the bank, but we took £10,000 worth of orders as a result of the show. Our first order came from Harvey Nichols for £3,500, which was a lot of money to us then,' said Monty.

The three directors who set up The Carpenters Workshop were also very precise in defining the market sector they would attack. Although all three originated from the food industry, they discovered from market research that there was a surprising gap in the market for quality wooden accessories for bathrooms and kitchens.

By good fortune, Marks & Spencer had made a similar discovery at around the same time. The leading retailers had scoured the UK and Europe for eighteen months to try and find a suitable manufacturer before coming across the Carpenters Workshop products at a gift fair in Birmingham.

Prior to placing a bulk order, Marks & Spencer decided on a trial run in twelve of its stores of the firm's co-ordinated bathroom range. It was the opportunity to break into a high volume business that Carpenters Workshop's directors had been waiting for – and indeed needed to survive.

To take full advantage of the opportunity, the company needed to gear up its modest production facilities. It took the gamble of moving into a much larger factory. 'It was fingers crossed time because, frankly, if that range hadn't gone well, it would have been goodbye Carpenters Workshop,' admitted Richard Martin, one of the founder directors.

Fortunately, the bathroom accessories sold well and Marks & Spencer followed up with a bulk order for the company's kitchen range. This included a pine wall clock, which Marks & Spencer was reluctant to sell because of disappointing results with a previous range of clocks. The pine clocks, however, instantly appealed to the buying public. They became the basis of what eventually turned out to be a million pound business in its own right for M&S.

'Until we came along, Marks & Spencer didn't sell clocks and had no intention of ever doing so. It now has a whole clock department which is turning over millions of pounds. We were given to believe that we had succeeded in capturing ten per cent of the whole UK wall clock market,' said Martin jubilantly.

In researching its market and coming up with a line that filled a market gap, The Carpenters Workshop found a quick route to bulk sales via one of the country's most prestigious multiple stores. Some experts question, however, whether a small business is wise to align its fortunes so closely with one predominant customer. It was a risk that The Carpenters Workshop was prepared to take.

One thing most small businesses would agree about, however, is that once their products have been accepted by a prestigious customer, their marketing problems are greatly reduced. Most small businesses regard it as an invaluable endorsement if Harrods or Selfridges, for example, smile on their products.

Having tested the market for her pressed flower pictures, Joanna Sheen admits she had only one aim in mind. 'We decided in a rather grandiose way that the only shop really worth selling to was Harrods,' she confessed.

Her husband camped outside the office of a Harrods' buyer and refused to be put off by statements to the effect that the buying season was over. Eventually, he succeeded in getting an audience, and the samples he took with him must have made an instant impression. The very next day the famous London store telephoned to place a £250 order. Since then the pictures have sold in their hundreds.

Sometimes a selling trip to Harrods can be a salutory experience. Bill Jones, one of the founding directors of Richard Broad Ltd., a company that makes traditional grandfather clocks, also believed in starting at the top end of the market. He succeeded at his first attempt in selling one of his firm's clocks to the London store. But while he was visiting the store he decided to do some market research and take a look at the grandfather clocks made by competitors on sale there.

He quickly came to the conclusion that the clocks his own company made fell short in quality. 'I went back a bit despondent,' he admitted. 'But it inspired us to improve our own models.'

The best market research is often personal experience. If you have difficulty in obtaining a product or service you badly need, the chances are hundreds of other people have undergone the same experience. You have probably identified a gap in the market which is waiting for some enterprising person to fill.

This is exactly what happened to Sue Jacoby. She and her family were planning a ski-ing holiday and she decided to hire some equipment for her children. 'We didn't want to pay the earth and we ended up getting some gear sent down from London. It was very tatty and thoroughly unsatisfactory. It only arrived two days before we were due to leave and there was a panic as to whether the children would have any ski clothes at all.'

It occurred to Sue that other families must have gone through the same nerve-racking experience. There appeared to be a hole in the market. Sue, who had previously skied competitively for her country, was very knowledgeable about how to get equipped for the slopes.

She decided to convert her expertise into a business offering advice to schoolchildren making their first trips to the ski slopes.

The business began modestly, but within a few years Sue was kitting out schoolchildren from over fifty schools. She was greatly helped by her husband, Martin, a former school teacher, who did a market survey of 780 schools to discover which of them sent ski-ing parties abroad and which of those required the service Sue's company offered.

Spotting a market gap while working for a travel firm was the spark that inspired Tony Scragg to set up his own business. As communications manager for the travel firm, Scragg wanted to find out how many callers were trying to get through at peak times. Often the firm's switchboard was jammed with inquiries, but he had no means of knowing how many potential customers were trying to get through or were perhaps giving up out of frustration.

He scanned the market for a system that would collect data about incoming calls and display the information instantly on a screen. In particular, he wanted to know how long callers were holding on, how many were giving up and how many were hitting the engaged tone.

He needed this information instantly, so that he could deploy staff to man the telephones at peak times, but not divert them from other important work when business was more slack.

His search for such a system was in vain, however. Most scanners of the kind he needed only collate data on outgoing calls. The only solution was to get someone to produce a custom-designed system. With the help of two telecommunications engineers, he managed to come up with a scanner that did the trick.

He and the two engineers were so pleased with the end result that they jointly formed a company to market the scanner. After only a year in operation, they could count many leading organizations and companies among their customers.

Most people would have considered the telecommunications industry, dominated by giant corporations, as a market that was pretty sewn up, but Scragg and his fellow directors proved that there are always market niches waiting to be filled by small businesses.

[99]

Farmer Andrew Curtis had a similar experience when he decided to feed his cows by computer. He selected one of several systems available on the market and built a bulk storage and feed cubicle to house all the electronics and to protect the animals and cattle cake from bad weather.

He was so pleased with the design he came up with for the integral feeding cabin that he decided to market it to other farmers. To his surprise and delight, he soon found that he had set in motion a flourishing business.

'We set what we thought was a high target to sell forty of the feeding cubicles in the first year. We achieved that in four months,' said Curtis.

Once the would-be entrepreneur has settled on a product line that market research indicates he will be able to sell in quantity for a profit, the next major decision is how to go about attracting the attention of potential customers.

There is a bewildering array of techniques available for communicating with the market place, some of them extremely expensive. 'Advertising is the best known form of communication,' says marketing consultant Ian Jennings, 'but by no means the only one. Press and public relations, sales literature, product packaging, point-of-sale display, exhibitions, sponsorship, personal recommendation and salesmanship are all part of the mix.

'There are no simple rules to follow. Different markets and methods of sale dictate the mix required. Consumer sales through retail outlets will be more dependent on advertising, package design and point-of-sale displays than say, industrial sales through distributors, which will depend on the quality of technical literature, catalogues and the service offered the customer.'

Exhibitions are a popular way for many small businesses to promote their products. They can be highly cost-effective, since the company's stand will be visible to a large number of potential customers at a single location. If it is a trade fair, the visitors are usually there because they have an inherent interest in the range of products on display.

But like many things, there is an art to exhibiting at a trade fairs that inexperienced businessmen often learn the hard way. A computer software company that had not been long in the business decided to demonstrate its unique capabilities at a major international trade fair.

Run by a small, but dedicated, team of entrepreneurs, the company was unable to spare the time or the manpower to organize and prepare its stand until the very last moment. As a result, the stand was still being erected late on the night before the opening day. At this very late stage, the firm discovered to its horror that the stand had been designed the wrong shape for the space available. It had to make hasty changes to the design that worked against the main theme of the message the company wanted to put across.

The company also discovered that it had been allocated a space that was at the end of a blind alley, well away from the main focus of attention of the exhibition. Even worse, a rival firm that was well established in the software business had a prime position and partially blocked the new firm's stand from general view.

But this was only the start of the software company's problems. With mounting frustration, it discovered that the nearest electricity socket was a long way from where its stand would be positioned. It did not have leads long enough to reach. Without a lot of Heath Robinson re-wiring, it was in danger of not being able to demonstrate the very capabilities it wanted to promote to potential customers.

All these last minute adjustments kept the stand staff up until the early hours of the opening day of the exhibition. When finally they managed to get the stand into some semblance of order, they were tired, dishevelled, and far from alert. The trickle of visitors who did find their way to the company's remote location were met with disgruntled and confused staff who found the eleventh-hour redesign of the stand impractical to work with.

In order to make it fit the available space, the company had cancelled the idea of a section where staff could sit and chat in a relaxed way to prospective customers. Instead, they had to talk to visitors over the counter. The visitors soon grew tired of having to stand about and be jostled. Consequently, the software company's tally of orders at the end of the exhibition was almost negligible and the morale and confidence of its staff had been badly damaged.

Fortunately, not every first-time exhibiter at a trade fair goes through such a nightmarish experience. Those who take the trouble to discuss with the trade fair organisers what they are going to get for their money and how they can best display their products to full advantage are likely to avoid many of the pitfalls.

Some local councils and trade associations organize trade fairs at which major companies exhibit the components that go into their products and invite small firms to put in tenders which might be competitive with the major companies' regular suppliers. There have been many cases where a major manufacturer sends halfway across the world at great expense for components which are being made by an industrious small business just down the road.

The sad truth is, however, that most large firms depend on bulk suppliers, that offer them enticing discounts, with which small firms cannot possibly compete. Most of the contracts major firms put the way of small firms tend to be the crumbs rather than the hoped-for bonanza.

Poor market research can often result in a company promoting a perfectly good product in the wrong way. This would almost certainly have happened to RDA Injection, a company set up to make electronic fuel injection systems for motor-cycles, if it hadn't sought the help of a marketing consultant.

Before going into business for himself, Richard Atkins, the firm's founder, had spent many years in the glamorous end of the car industry, working for Jaguar among others, on developing fuel injection systems for sports cars. While working for one engineering group, he led a team that developed injection systems for Lotus.

The patent rights to the system were later sold to a West German company, which left Atkins without a job. He decided to set up his own company, operating initially from home, to service the systems already sold.

This inevitably provided limited opportunities. So Atkins cast around for other market openings and the motor-cycle trade caught his attention. 'There was a huge potential market on the motor-cycle side, particularly for the larger machines, because nobody in the world was fitting fuel injection equipment to them. At that time, it was a completely unknown concept for motor-bikes,' enthused Atkins. 'After doing a few sums and a bit of basic research, we found to our amazement that bigger bikes were doing in the region of 30 to 40 miles to the gallon, whereas 30 years ago they were doing from 70 to 75 mph. We came to the conclusion that modern bikes were very badly carburetted.'

This indicated to Atkins that he should market his fuel injection system to motor-cycle owners by stressing its ability to save on fuel. As it turned out, this would have been a false trail.

At the suggestion of the British Technology Group, a government-sponsored organization, to whom Atkins had gone for financial backing and advice, RDA Injection decided to explore the market in greater depth with the aid of marketing consultant Ian Jennings.

The first question Jennings sought to answer was what it would take to persuade motor-cycling enthusiasts, who spend up to £4,000 or £5,000 for their machines, to fork out an extra £400 for the fuel injection kit. 'I came to the conclusion very rapidly that the reason most people own big bikes is that they like to live dangerously,' said Jennings. 'They really just want the thrill of being able to go fast and to leave the other guy behind. It was clear that the whole marketing strategy needed to be built around that.'

Atkins had developed a system that made huge improvements in the fuel consumption, which could be fitted to existing machines at little cost or effort. But Jennings convinced him that in marketing terms, fuel efficiency was not the main factor to promote. 'It became clear that what we had to push was power,' concluded Atkins.

He and Jennings undertook an intensive tour of the main UK importers of Japanese bikes to spread the word that the do-it-yourself injection kit could give their machines the extra thrust that every motor-cycling enthusiast yearns for.

They also visited the annual British Motor Cycle Federation rally at Peterborough, which attracts motor-cycle enthusiasts in their tens of thousands. They distributed 2,000 leaflets there, which resulted in an enormous number of inquiries, ten per cent of which were converted to hard orders – an unusually high ratio.

This was followed up by a London press conference to launch the product, which resulted in write-ups in specialist publications circulating in Britain and abroad. From these came inquiries from Holland, Sweden, Denmark, Canada and the USA.

Market research should not grind to a halt once a small business has established a successful product line. We live in unpredictable times in which once-flourishing markets can vanish almost overnight. The small business entrepreneur needs to be ever-vigilant and to monitor changes in market forces which may present a serious threat to the viability of his company. He must always be prepared to adjust his marketing policy or diversify into new product lines if the need arises.

When in the early 1980s it looked as though the recession was going to scupper his previously flourishing inflatable dinghy business, Jock Henshaw scoured the horizon for less vulnerable product lines and came up with an inflatable pipe stopper and an air-lift for raising stricken cows to their feet.

Both product lines were far removed from the boating business, but they were nevertheless based on the same basic technology Henshaw had developed for his inflatable craft.

Up until March, 1980, he couldn't turn out his small boats fast enough to keep up with demand. Then suddenly the sales bonaza died out without warning. 'It just went absolutely dead and we didn't sell a boat for weeks,' recalled Henshaw. 'We suddenly found ourselves producing for stock and at one point we had sixty boats piled up in a shed. In hindsight, we didn't put the brake on fast enough. The raw materials were still coming in and had to be paid for.'

It soon became apparent to Henshaw that if he was to survive, he needed something to tide him over the recession. As luck would have it, he was approached by an inventor who had come up with the idea of an inflatable pipe-stopper, which was like a rubber tyre with a membrane in the middle to seal it. Applied to the end of a section of pipe it could be used to test for leaks under pressure.

Henshaw gratefully grasped the opportunity to diversify into a new market. But the invention needed refining and it took six months and £33,000 of investment to arrive at the finished product. With his bank manager already showing signs of disquiet over his escalating overdraft, it was a testing time for Henshaw.

But the end product proved infinitely more practical than conventional metal stoppers. Henshaw sold £60,000 worth of the inflatable stoppers within the first six months of launching them on the market. He eventually struck up a deal with a distributor, but the market proved to be limited as a lot of those who bought the stoppers subsequently hired them out to other firms.

It was clear to Henshaw that another product was needed to carry him through the recession. Again, he was lucky. This time he was asked by a local vet if he could make a device to hoist sick or injured cows off the ground. Cows often collapse as a result of such diseases as milk fever contracted after calving or simply slip and injure themselves. Conventional methods of raising them off the ground, using clamps and tackle, are not very humane and can cause additional injuries.

Putting his inventive mind to the task, Henshaw came up with a simple inflatable cylinder, which when placed under the stricken cow can be blow up to gently raise the animal to its feet. This time the investment in a prototype cost less than £100 and sales were soon brisk.

Because of their limited markets, neither product was a runaway success. But sales were sufficiently buoyant for Henshaw to keep his workers employed until the economic tide flowed in his favour again. When the boat trade picked up once more, he went back to making dinghies, the mainstay of his business.

EXPORTING

Too many small businessmen adopt a very blinkered attitude to marketing. They tend to confine their trading initially to the region they operate from, in the mistaken belief that it is the best policy to expand the market in easy stages as the business builds up. What they tend to overlook is that if they don't generate enough sales, they won't have a business for very long. To achieve the volume of sales necessary to sustain a viable business usually means casting a very wide net.

Testing the market locally is probably a sensible idea.

Pauline Ralph received encouraging feedback when she visited local souvenir shops to sound out reaction to the prototype musical box she had made. But once she had received a positive response, she wasted no time expanding both nationally and internationally. Her company now exports to numerous countries and among the forty-five different styles of musical box being produced is a range of New England miniature houses specially geared for the US market.

The most successful small businesses are invariably those who go for export markets at an early stage in their development. Some jump in at the deep end right from the word go. Valerie Burrell has built up her successful knitwear company almost entirely on export orders.

Shortly after setting up her company, she went to a meeting of a local export association. One of the officials was about to go to the US to show buyers samples of products made by some of the association's members. He took some of Burrell's knitwear with him.

'They were a sell-out,' recalled Burrell. 'I have only ever sold a small proportion in this country because everything we make is always totally taken up with exports. We've never been able to fulfil the orders we could get. I've had to turn away £20,000 orders sometimes.'

Practically all the company's turnover is derived from exports to the US, where there is not the same tradition of home knitting as there is in this country. The Americans pay handsomely for the exclusive designs and for the handicraft that goes into them. Hand-knitted garments are a status symbol in the US and the more expensive they are the more the Americans clamour to buy them.

But not all Burrell's exporting activities went so smoothly. For years she exported very successfully to Japan, building up an annual market worth £60,000. Then suddenly demand fell off dramatically. After making inquiries, she discovered to her horror that her designs were being copied in Hong Kong and then sold on to the Japanese market.

There was very little she could do about it. She was advised that legal action, even if it were successful, would probably cost her more than any compensation she was likely to receive.

She approached a new agent in Japan to try to sell her knitwear under a different brand name, but she was advised it would be best if she forgot all about the Japanese market for several years. 'The Japanese agent suggested that I wait awhile because I had lost face. The Japanese hate victims and losers and if you've been taken for a ride, you've lost face,' said Burrell, amused by the irony and injustice of her position.

It is understandable that many start-up entrepreneurs fight shy of going for export markets. If there are problems attached to finding the right home market, they are multiplied many times when it comes to exporting. When things go wrong a long distance from a company's base, it can be a real nightmare trying to sort them out, unless the company has an agent located abroad.

Building up a healthy export market can make all the difference to a company's growth pattern, but achieving overseas sales can be fraught with pitfalls.

There are three main factors first-time exporters need to get right if they are to succeed. These are finding the right market for a particular product; ensuring the product is priced right for overseas; and making sure that you are going to get paid at the end of the day.

The most common mistake made by first-time exporters is that they fail to do the necessary market research. They assume that, because their products are selling well on the home market, they will automatically achieve good sales abroad – in France, for example.

George Raybould, chairman of a regional association of exporting firms, warns: 'There may already be a French manufacturer making similar products that sell at a cheaper price. You've got to look at the market as a whole.

'If you're selling grandfather clocks, for example, I don't think China would be the place. It would probably be better to concentrate on the American market and to a lesser extent, South Africa and possibly West Germany.'

On the other hand, it can be very rewarding if you do manage to break into a new market which on the face of it doesn't offer much prospect. A firm that makes vehicles for recreation parks succeeded in selling a consignment of go-karts to China – not the most promising market for such a product.

Raybould suggests, however, that the first-time exporter should choose a 'soft market' to begin with to gain confidence. He lists the Netherlands, West Germany, Denmark, Norway and Sweden as countries that are pro-British and therefore less likely to be 'a hard sale'.

France, by contrast, is a notoriously difficult market to break into, mainly because it insists on use of the French language for labelling, invoices and contracts.

A lot of information about the peculiarities of different foreign markets can be obtained from the British Overseas Trade Board. It has an information desk for each country and records the names of companies all over the world which might just be looking for the very product you make.

Inexperienced exporters also tend to leave too small a margin when pricing their products for overseas markets. They believe naively that if they price at £75 a product that has cost them £50 to make, they will make a tidy profit. They grossly under-estimate the cost of getting their products on to the foreign markets.

'Just take selling to America,' says Raybould. 'You've got to pay American import duty, plus customs clearance charges, plus the cost of shipment and delivery to the customer over there. To cover all that, your £50 product probably needs to sell for £200.'

Many first-time exporters become so over-awed at winning a substantial overseas order, they don't stop to think how they are going to get their money. They rely on the goodwill of the foreign customer. Such vagueness can be fatal. Companies which put too much faith in verbal promises often end up going out of business.

'You've got to decide whether you want the buyer to pay before the goods are shipped or afterwards,' cautions Raybould. 'If it's afterwards, is it thirty days after the date of shipment or the date of the invoice, or what? Is the customer going to provide an irrevocable letter of credit?'

Most of the large clearing banks run an exporter's scheme similar to a factoring service, which guarantees a high percentage of an invoice value as soon as it is despatched.

Despite the availability of such safeguards, many inexperienced entrepreneurs rush into exporting without considering the risks they are taking. The market that has a special fascination for many is the oil-rich Middle East, with its inflated reputation for turning entrepreneurs into millionaires overnight. If the experience of one unfortunate entrepreneur is anything to go by, it is just as easy to lose a fortune.

Colin Bailey thought he had it made when his small export company secured a £1 million order for construction materials from a firm in Jordan. But his celebration was premature. After a series of heart-breaking setbacks, he ended up having to file for bankruptcy.

Apart from the vagaries of doing business in the Middle East, Bailey blamed bad advice from solicitors and accountants for the ruination of his business. Even a cable to King Hussein of Jordan failed to save him from disaster.

The story that led to Bailey's downfall began in 1977 when together with a partner he set up his export business. It occurred to him that there was money to be made from acting as a go-between for construction firms in the Middle East and manufacturers in the UK. He flew to Jordan where he was introduced to a Korean contractor.

Several days later he flew home with a contract ostensibly worth £1 million to supply construction materials for a new township that was being built on the banks of the Dead Sea. Baily placed orders with UK firms for the first phase of the contract and arranged for the materials to be shipped to Jordan.

The deal should have been covered by a letter of credit which would have guaranteed that Bailey's firm would get its money and that the Korean contractor would get its goods. Unfortunately, Bailey's company submitted the necessary documents to make the letter of credit valid too late.

The bank involved was obliged to abide by the rules and checked with the Korean firm whether it would stick by the agreement, but it refused to pay up. Bailey made several attempts to get his money, but to no avail. There was no way he could see of getting the goods back, so he ended up with £26,000 worth of debts and his firm was forced into liquidation.

Some time later, Bailey came into a small inheritance from an aunt who had died. This enabled him to start a new company. This time he went into business on his own. Undaunted by past experience, Bailey again set out for Jordan, where he was introduced to a Jordanian representative of a construction firm who came highly recommended by the commercial attaché at the British Embassy.

Again, Bailey secured what appeared to be a major order. This time he was appointed sole agent for construction materials for a £25 million project to build the new headquarters of a leading Iraqi newspaper. The UK element of the deal was alone worth £2.5 million.

Bailey's contract for the first phase of the deal was worth £600,000. His company stood to gain a five per cent commission from the transaction. Recalling his previous misfortune, he was careful to check with solicitors that the contract was foolproof. He was assured that it was water-tight.

A few weeks later, however, the war between Iran and Iraq broke out and Bailey lost contact with the Jordanian businessman. Over the period of a year he sent telex messages and letters imploring the Jordanian to stick to the terms of the contract. But he got nowhere.

In the meantime, he was forced to borrow additional working capital to keep the business afloat. He took out a loan with a finance company at a fixed interest of twenty-four per cent with his home as security. He flew to Jordan ten times to try to get the contract honoured, running up debts of £25,000. Yet he was no nearer getting his money.

Eventually, Baily did manage to track down the Jordanian businessman in Amsterdam. The Jordanian gave him a cheque for £5,000 and a verbal assurance that the rest would follow soon. The cheque bounced three times.

Bailey later discovered that the contract was not so water-tight after all. It was only covered by Jordanian law and was not actionable in Britain. Legal advisers told him that he would have to put up £2,000 security before his case could be proceeded with. He was reluctant to get any further into debt.

To add to Bailey's dilemma, he discovered that due to an oversight his business had not been registered as a limited liability company. It meant that when he went into liquidation he was personally liable for the company's debts. He lost everything.

Bailey's was an extreme case, but many small businessmen have tasted the bitter experience of trying to open up markets in the Middle East where reality invariably falls short of promise.

There is a widespread misconception among inexperienced Middle East-bound businessmen that the area represents easy pickings and that big profits can be made without much investment in time, money or energy.

What many businessmen tackling the Middle East for the first time tend to overlook is that it has become a buyer's market. According to one consultant familiar with the Middle East scene: 'The decision-makers in the Middle East realize that to a large extent they were ripped off in the late 1960s and early 1970s and are now much more stringent in their commercial dealings. Also, a lot of major developments have already been done.'

A survey among businessmen who regularly travel to the Middle East concluded that cultural empathy was the most important prerequisite for operating there successfully. Any businessmen venturing into the Middle East for the first time who does not bear this in mind is very likely to return home empty handed.

One of the main pitfalls is the failure to recognize that Middle East people have an entirely different concept of space and time to Westerners. Tying Middle East businessmen down to a fixed appointment can be a nightmare. Newcomers touring the Middle East are advised to try to stick to a schedule, but not to fret if things go awry.

It is not unusual to arrive for a firm appointment with a Middle East executive only to find he is not even in the country. Advises a regular Middle East visitor: 'Be patient. It is absolutely vital. They don't intend to be rude and it is very easy to lose your cool when you're tired from travelling.'

Once having got an appointment, the visiting businessman will often be horrified to discover that he has to conduct his transactions in a room full of people. It is not unusual for a Middle East executive to hold court with a whole group of hopeful visitors. Insisting on a private meeting will only antagonize the host, from whom it is hoped to secure a contract.

Middle East concepts of courtesy and respect can be very confusing to outsiders. Suggests the consultant: 'Don't confuse courtesy and hospitality with sincerity. The visiting businessman will do well to assess what he has achieved at the end of each day. The host country's friendliness may leave him with a comfortable feeling that things are going well, but he should ask himself whether he has really made any progress.'

The Middle East novice will soon be disabused of the popular view that business can be done there out of a suitcase. The big orders nearly always go to those who have on-the-spot facilities and give the impression of a degree of permanence. To get contracts, it is necessary to have constant follow-up. Middle Easterners are notorious for failing to answer letters or respond to telexes.

Most Middle East veterans regard it as essential to have a local agent. He will be able, among other things, to keep the businessman informed about new projects before they are publicly announced. He will also have inside knowledge about who the key decision-makers are when it comes to major contracts.

The agent will be familiar with the ever-changing regulations in each country. The sudden introduction of a regulation that makes it mandatory to submit all proposals for public sector work in Arabic, for example, can cause havoc to the businessman caught unawares.

Customs regulations, too, are frequently changed. For example, if a country's government feels that sufficient quantities of a certain range of products are available within the region, it can ban their importation overnight. A good agent will alert the businessman to such dangers.

But choosing the right agent is very important. The Middle East is swarming with people who offer to be agents. Many of them lack the contacts and influence they claim. It is best to check with the British Embassy or the local expatriate community before making a decision.

The issue that most troubles newcomers to the Middle East is the vexed problem of bribes and commissions. Middle East veterans draw a clear distinction between a commission and a bribe. It is generally considered to be above board to pay a commission for information or to ensure that your tender does not get overlooked. It is advisable, however, not to offer a bribe to ensure that a contract is guaranteed to the exclusion of other competitive tenders.

It should always be remembered, however, that Middle Easterners are all traders by nature. Wheeling and dealing is in their blood.

Authority is centralized in most Middle East companies. The head of a firm usually insists on meeting business contacts personally. By the same token, Middle East executives expect to deal with chiefs, not Indians. They are usually not interested in negotiating with business representatives who lack the authority to make decisions. And although they take their time in awarding contracts, they expect the goods to be delivered tomorrow once an agreement has been reached.

A new, highly educated generation of Arabs is now beginning to appear on the scene, who give the impression that the differences between the Middle East and the Western world are vanishing. These knowledgeable executives are given positions of great authority in their firms because it is regarded as undignified to make them climb up through the ranks as business graduates are made to do in the West.

It is important to remember that although they may have degrees from Harvard or the London School of Economics, they will almost certainly lack practical experience.

Case Study A

The Perfect Sundial

When Gwyn Lawrence decided to set up a business to produce the perfect sundial, he had little idea how much basic research he was going to have to do. His task was made all the harder since he came cold to sundial technology. Trained as a diesel fitter, he was quite skilled at putting things together, but he had never before attempted to make anything from scratch. Nor did his previous work experience as a technician and driver for several pop groups stand him in very good stead.

He first hit on the idea that there could be a market for sundials during a trip to California. He had been working solidly for five years without a break, latterly as a technician for the Welsh National Opera, and he went to California for a change of scenery.

While there, he was impressed by the number of gardens that were without sundials in what was an ideal climate for them.

Back home again, Lawrence searched for reference books on sundials, but found there were very few. He spent a lot of time touring museums, such as the Greenwich Maritime Museum and the British Museum in London. Eventually, he put a brief together, which in hindsight he described as 'incredibly naive'.

'I wanted a durable, accurate, aesthetic sundial and it had to be round,' he recalled with a tinge of amusement. There were only three parts to be made – the brass dial face, the slate to mount it on and the gnomon (or indicator). In theory, it should have been straightforward.

On reflection, Lawrence realized that he did the whole exercise the wrong way round. He should have looked first at the manufacturing problems and then asked a designer to come up with a prototype to take account of them. In fact, he first designed his perfect model and then explored how best to manufacture it. That was when his troubles really began.

'I went to all the North Wales slate quarries and none of them could produce a thirteen inch circular slate face eonomically. Then I went to a tooling company. They could make me a diamond tipped core drill to cut the circle, but it was going to cost me an arm and a leg.'

After a lot more investigation, Lawrence found an engineering company that helped him to make a less expensive drill. He also tracked down the only man in his part of the world who could work with slate in the round. Eventually, he ended up with the right shape slate, even though the slating industry told him that what he was seeking was impossible.

The next problem arose when the brass pieces for the sundial face arrived. They were slightly oval rather than the requested circular shape. The difference was not obvious, but when combined with the perfectly round slates they did not fit. The suppliers insisted the brass circles were as accurate as modern technology could achieve. So Lawrence had to find someone to turn the ovals into circles.

The next snag came when Lawrence needed to etch the Roman numerals on to the brass. To achieve the effect he wanted, Lawrence opted for an ultra-modern chemical milling process, which, unlike more conventional milling techniques, puts no stress on the metal. The process is used in the electronics industry to make printed circuit boards.

The process is a closely-guarded secret among the companies that have developed it. Because it is such a modern process, there are no reference books about it. But Lawrence eventually managed to acquire sufficient knowledge of the process to do it the way he wanted.

That just left the gnomon. Inevitably, the pattern of setbacks continued. Lawrence had decided to make the sundials accurate to five degrees of latitude. He designed ten different models, so that customers could purchase the sundial most appropriate to the latitude at which they lived. He bought time on a university's mainframe computer to calculate the angle of the gnomon for each latitude.

He opted first to make the gnomons from a casting, but the quality he could achieve fell short of what he was seeking. The only alternative was to use computerized numerically controlled milling machines. A company that undertakes sophisticated milling for the motor industry took on the contract.

So, finally, Lawrence's perfect sundial, designed to last 500 years, was a reality. But two years after setting out on his quest, he was not at all sure it had all been worth the effort. 'No individual should ever get trapped into doing original research and development. That should be left to big companies and the government, whatever people say about inventors in back yards,' concluded Lawrence.

But what made Lawrence question the wisdom of his quest even more seriously was the sudden realization that he had failed to discover whether there was a sufficiently large market for the sundials to justify all the painstaking research he had put into them.

He obtained £60,000 under the government's guaranteed loan scheme and a further £15,000 from a development agency to go into production, but it soon became apparent that sales were not going to match his expectations. Eventually, economic reality began to chip away at his ideals. Looking at it pragmatically, it was obvious that the sundials were far too expensive to make. They were enormously complicated to produce and there was a lot of wastage of the raw material, since the circles started off as squares. In addition, sundials are generally given as presents and sell better in gift shops than at garden centres. However, the sundials Lawrence was making tended to be too heavy for foreign visitors to take on board aeroplanes and were too expensive to buy for the average tourist.

Taking all these factors into account, Lawrence decided to make a range of smaller, less expensive, square-faced sundials. He also dispensed with the idea of making them accurate to the appropriate latitude. The realization dawned that people who buy sundials do not use them primarily to tell the time, but rather to enhance the appearance of their gardens. In any case, the sundials he made were accurate to solar time, which has little resemblance to the artificial time by which most of us live.

If Lawrence had spent as much effort on market research as he did on product research, he would not have had to learn such lesssons the hard way.

Case Study B

A House of Glass

The House of Marbles started life as a company that was struggling to make a living from selling toys. The only line that seemed to go well was board games. So the firm's three directors decided to concentrate on these. They broadened the range to include games of strategy based on those originally played by the ancient Egyptians and eighth century Vikings.

The board games all required small marbles which were plain in colour and not very exciting to look at. In order to introduce a little more sparkle to the games, the firm's founders searched all over the world for more colourful varieties of marbles.

The marbles they eventually ended up with proved to be more appealing to their young customers than the actual games. From then on the business really started to take off.

'Instead of being a company that was one hundred per cent games, it became fifty per cent marbles,' explained Bill Bavin, one of its directors. 'Over the years we've developed more and more interesting colours and sizes. We now make marbles that are collectors' items,'

When demand began to outstrip supply, the company explored the idea of producing its own marbles via a local glass manufacturer. When the costings were done, however, it proved to be too expensive, since profit margins on individual marbles are minute. 'It's the cost of gas in this country that is so prohibitive,' lamented Bavin, referring to the power needs for the ultra-hot furnaces used in glass-making.

The solution was to have the marbles made in the US, where gas is a lot cheaper. The company acquired its own rolling machines in West Virginia, which were capable of turning out two million marbles a day in a twenty-four-hour operation.

But the ultra-efficiency of the US marble machines threw up another problem. Even with the high demand it had created, there was little prospect of the company finding a market for the vast numbers of marbles the US machines were capable of spilling out.

To make the investment worthwhile, it was necessary to create an additional market for the marbles. Searching their brains for such a market, the directors hit on the idea of trying to convince aerosol manufacturers that glass marbles would be a practical and much cheaper substitute for steel bearings as agitators.

'In all paint sprays there's a small ball inside that charges around and mixes the paint. They always used to be steel balls. Now, ninety per cent of all agitators in spray cans are glass,' said Bavin.

The American machines can only produce marbles in a single colour. As the company's reputation grew as one of the foremost producers of glass marbles, it felt the need to make the multi-coloured spiral-patterned variety invented by the Victorians that are the delight of every schoolchild.

These can only be produced by hand, so the House of Marbles opened its own glass studios for this purpose. To justify the expense of such a labour-intensive operation the firm branched out into other types of glassware.

Its products were eventually to find their way into 1,000 toy and giftware shops, including such upmarket stores as Harrods. Around thirty per cent of its turnover was eventually to come from exports.

The company's diversification strategy eventually turned full circle. It returned to selling toys, including a range of dinosaurs and insects made from laminated wood, imported from Japan. The company is a graphic example of the fact that in order to survive in today's fluctuating economic climate, small businesses need to have the flexibility to adapt to changing market trends.

Case Study C

Following His Nose

Until 1978, Ian Mitchell had been a bit of a Jack-of-all-trades. He had worked in the building and electronics industries and he had even tried running a ski school in Spain. Then his life changed dramtically.

'My whole philosophy of life changed. I became a vegetarian and I was very sensitive to what I should eat and what I shouldn't. It was just one of those stages you go through in life,' he recalled.

As a result of shopping at health food shops, Mitchell and his wife Judy hit on the idea of making natural skin and hair care products to sell on the open market. They started modestly, working from two rooms above a funeral parlour. 'We got help from a consultant chemist in Cambridge who was sympathetic to our ideas. Judy, who had once been a beauty consultant, used to make the products and I would go around the health stores taking the orders,' explained Mitchell.

In 1979 they formed a company called Applewoods on a £1,000 bank overdraft. 'We realized we wouldn't be able to compete with the large companies, because we didn't have the financial resources to produce the advertising and all the other back-up that is required. We had to rely solely on point-of-sale presentations and the actual product,' said Mitchell.

This meant taking special care over the design of the packaging. They employed freelance designers to come up with distinctive wrapping reflecting the specialised nature of the products. 'We had to ensure that our products stood out on the shelves,' said Mitchell.

Eventually some of the big London stores began to take notice of Applewoods' products and started ordering them, often to their own special requirements. As a result, the company moved away steadily from natural skin products and more into giftware, such as novelty soaps and gift-packed shampoo sets.

'Fairly early on I became acutely aware that one of the plus points to products in this market is fragrance,' said Mitchell. 'There are two things that normally sell a product – what it looks like and a sense of touch. We have the added advantage in our business of the sense of smell. So I realized I had to have two things – a good presentation and a good fragrance. All the ingredients are still natural ingredients. We never lost that'.

Another factor that caused the Mitchells to change direction was the realization that skin and hair care products offered limited potential for extending the company's range. But by following their nose and expanding their product range to include anything that involved fragrance, the Mitchells opened up a virtual Pandora's Box of possible products, from scented drawer liners to scented note-paper. The range was eventually expanded to 400 different items.

The novelty soap lines blossomed into a variety of ranges, including alphabet soaps which spell out people's names, to zodiac soaps, number soaps and soaps with days of the week on them. Constantly let down by its suppliers, Applewoods eventually started manufacturing its own soap. That paved the way for entry into another lucrative market – customised soap for hotels and major chain stores.

The company became one of the few firms in the country able to produce small runs of customised soap by semi-automated methods. It succeeded in making it viable to produce as few as 2,500 tablets of soap at a time.

The Mitchells were careful to cultivate both ends of the market with their branded lines. They developed a fashionable range packaged in primary colours to appeal to the young set and a classic range for the more traditional taste. 'The classic range is in deep rich colours and fragrancies. Burgundy is matched with a traditional rose and deep blue with geranium, another traditional fragrance,' elaborated Mitchell.

6

THE TECHNOLOGY-SHY
ENTREPRENEUR

The Good Sense of Investing in New Technology

IN a courageous crusade to keep Britain's lace industry alive, John Heather has invested over £1 million in the latest technology for his Nottingham-based company. He has installed eight computer-controlled knitting looms, costing around £150,000 each, to produce miles of delicate lace that turns lingerie into creations of graceful fashion.

A lot of people would say Heather has left it too late to save Britain's declining lace industry and that in any case lace-making is a craft that cannot be automated. He is determined to prove them wrong and in so doing provide a lesson for all technology-shy entrepreneurs.

It takes a lot of courage to invest large sums of money into a business that is in a declining market. But Heather firmly believes that installing modern technology is the best way to save many of Britain's ailing firms. In his view, it is the only way they are going to be able to compete with their foreign rivals.

Small business entrepreneurs tend to shy away from modern technology for a number of reasons. The main one is cost. Although there are a number of government grants available, installing new manufacturing equipment is an exorbitantly expensive affair and at the end of the day the business has got to make enough profit to justify such enormous investments. Small businessmen also tend to turn their back on modern technology because they believe they are getting into realms they don't understand. For many, computers and automation are a complete mystery and they are reluctant to get embroiled in techniques they cannot grasp.

Added to that, there is a strong conviction that automation inevitably results in contraction of the workforce. Many small businesses have been built on the loyalty of dedicated employees and the owner understandably doesn't wish to appear callous by shedding the very people who have led to his success for automated processes he has no guarantee will work for his company.

Heather believes, however, that firms, both large and small, have little option but to introduce modern technology if they are to survive. He has watched the steady decline of the lace industry and sees computerized equipment as the last-ditch hope. In the early 1920s, the British lace industry, centred in Nottingham, supported around 300 manufacturers and wholesalers. Today there are barely thirty companies left.

Britain has allowed its former markets to be stolen from it by manufacturers in the Far East, not, in Heather's view, because of the ecomomies of cheap labour, as is popularly believed, but because other countries saw more readily the sense of introducing modern technology.

Heather maintains that if Britain's lace industry had only possessed the foresight to make the substantial investments necessary to upgrade its machinery, it could have taken on and beaten its Far East rivals. The same technology, he argues, is available to everyone. Companies everywhere are now all governed by the same rules of the game.

'Machine-made lace has been with us for 200 years and I

don't see any reason why it should go into further decline,' asserts Heather. 'It's a craft industry and like a lot of craft industries, it must learn to survive in spite of the pace of change and new technology.' With well over thirty years in the industry, Heather has the vision, which so many other entrepreneurs lack, to see how it can be achieved.

His main concern is that craftsmen are leaving the industry in droves, taking with them skills developed over centuries. He is convinced young people must be persuaded to enter the industry before the skills vanish for good. He spends a lot of his time making speeches at local schools and colleges to convince young people that there is still a future in the industry.

To secure that future for them, Heather is demonstrating the courage of his convictions by switching to computer-controlled looms. The machines are made by Karl Meyer in West Germany, the sole supplier of such equipment. Walking between the avenues of chattering looms, weaving their intricate patterns to computer commands is an eerie experience. Operators sit gazing into visual display units that answer to German language instructions. The demand for such equipment in the UK is so insignificant, the German manufacturers haven't bothered to come up with an English-language program.

The automated system achieves around seventy per cent efficiency, compared to forty per cent with the former chain-driven machines. A major pattern change on one of the old machines could involve up to three weeks' downtime at a cost to the company of £3,000 a week. The same change over with computer control takes only a few days.

With such efficient machinery to back him up, Heather feels a lot more confident about the future than when he took over the running of the company on the retirement of the company's founder. The company was in a weak position financially and a very difficult trading period lay ahead throughout the 1970s, when lace, for the most part, was out of fashion.

Department stores were not interested in selling high fashion garments. The bulk demand was for inferior quality lace. All that changed in 1979, however. The company's traditional markets all started trading up and Heather, who had already made up his mind to upgrade the quality of his products, decided to seize the opportunity to modernize his manufacturing facilities.

'It was a brave decision,' admits Heather, 'but most of us had been in the business for a good many years and we had nowhere else to go except stay in the lace industry. We were committed to it and we didn't like what was happening to it. We decided we were going to produce the best lace we possibly could, using the best yarns and the best machinery. While we accepted that lace was a craft industry, we realized we had to deliver craft in volume.'

It is understandable that small business entrepreneurs shudder at the prospect of making large investments in technology. But those who have the foresight to do so invariably reap the rewards. Michael Jordan runs a spiral staircase company which grew out of his father's blacksmith firm. The business expanded to the point where Jordan felt the need for a computer-aided design system to reduce the amount of time-consuming manual work being done by his draughtsmen.

The fees being charged by expert consultants were beyond Jordan's means. So he decided to seek the help of a local technical college. The students there were only too delighted to be given a real-life project to tackle and came up with a system tailor-made for Jordan's needs.

The facility enabled Jordan to display different design configurations at the touch of a button. His customers could be shown computer graphic variations to standard staircase models in a matter of seconds, leaving the firm's draughtsmen free to spend their time on more creative pursuits.

It is easier to justify the heavy expense of keeping up-to-date with the most modern equipment in the case of companies that are built around a technological product. During the height of the recession, Derek Hews gambled that the upturn had to be around the corner and he invested in high productivity equipment, including a £140,000 laser trimming machine. He speculated that when the upturn came, his company, making thin film resistors for the electronics industry, would be required to work flat out as the demand for its products quickened.

It was the hardest decision he had ever had to make. 'To sign a cheque for £140,000 in the depth of a recession is not the easiest of things to do,' he said. 'I had many sleepless nights because the order book was shrinking all the time.'

But the gamble paid off. When business did eventually pick up again, Hews' company was poised to take full advantage and was able to steal a march on rival firms who had retrenched during the recession.

Mike Revill is another entrepreneur who has put his faith in state of the art technology to ensure success. Using some of the latest paint spraying and oven-curing technology, his company puts the finishing touches to a whole range of products and components. 'We're a bit like a laundry,' explained Revill. 'Instead of taking in dirty sheets, we take in sheets of metal and send them out with a coating on them.'

This is an over-simplified explanation of the company's operations. In its early days, the business did little more than apply a coat of paint to metal parts. It eventually, however, ended up using the very latest equipment and earned itself an almost unparalleled reputation for coating electronic components, which calls for a high degree of precision.

Many of the firm's 100 or more customers are leading electronics groups, such as Thorn EMI, Racal and British Aerospace. The company put the finishing touches to computer components used in the guidance system for NASA's shuttle programme, as a result of work it received through Thorn EMI.

It took twenty years for Revill's company to reach its position of pre-eminence in the industrial finishes market and he met with a good many setbacks along the way. 'You couldn't describe us as having a meteoric rise to success by any stretch of the imagination,' he said.

One of the setbacks occurred when Thorn EMI ran into problems with a revolutionary new body scanner. Revill's company had been involved in coating components for the instrument and the loss of that market was a severe blow.

However, word of Revill's precision work had reached other parts of the Thorn EMI empire and his company was soon being asked to carry out similar work on other components. Thorn EMI had been unable to find another firm in the country that could match Revill's skills.

The company steadily clawed its way back to profitability, building up to an annual turnover of around £500,000. It invested £100,000 in updating its equipment, including installation of a 40 ft hot air tunnel oven for improving the powder coating processes in which the company specializes. The investment was an affirmation of Revill's belief that to stay on top of a market, it is necessary to employ modern techniques.

He has set an example other small business entrepreneurs are often reluctant to follow, but technology-shy firms are beginning to get assistance from an unlikely quarter – academic institutions. Most universities and polytechnics have vast resources with commercial potential locked away that never get fully utilized.

Recognizing the wastefulness of the situation, a number of them have set up companies to sell their skills and resources on the open market. It is one of those solutions that brings great advantages to all concerned. The universities generate badly needed cash to improve their facilities at a time of severe cutbacks in government funding. The small businesses, which are strapped for cash and can't afford to buy in expensive expertise, are able to make use of resources which otherwise would be denied them.

The development has been slow to catch on because academic and commercial cultures make unhappy bedfellows. An academic, for example, believes that knowledge should be universally available. A business consultant, on the other hand, regards it as a strategic resource which often should be guarded with the utmost secrecy.

Plymouth Polytechnic overcame this problem when it set up a commercial enterprise by ensuring that it was run by an independent board and in commercial premises that were outside the college campus. Professional managers and consultants were recruited to run the company and were offered the incentive of a personal stake in the enterprise. The company was set up with two main divisions – a consultancy to help small businesses operate more efficiently and an information technology division, which makes use of a national network of computer experts to advise firms on how to introduce modern techniques.

Robin Chater, who was recruited to run the consultancy side, made no bones about the fact that the company had commercial, not philanthropic aims. The company set out to make a profit, but in doing so it was trying to bring aid to many beleaguered small businesses.

'Nearly all higher educational institutions have tried at some time or other to establish an enterprise company,' said Chater, 'but many of these consulting companies have been run by academics, who haven't been particularly motivated to run them commercially. They often see it as a glorified licensing body. They all tend to be rather passive.'

Plymouth Poly has been able to chart a different course as a result of a change in the law. At one time it was illegal for polytechnics to set up an enterprise company with an independent set of finances. That is no longer the case.

In attempting to take advantage of the change in the law, Plymouth Poly looked at ways in which its facilities could be better utilized to earn funds to be ploughed back into the college. To avoid the clash of cultures between academic and commercial outlooks, it established a totally separate company with the freedom to operate in accordance with commercial dictates.

Chater described the Plymouth venture as 'a pathfinding enterprise' and rejoiced in the amount of resources placed at his disposal. 'There are 400 lecturers and professional staff at the Polytechnic, huge resources in the laboratories, teleconferencing facilities, all under-utilized,' he pointed out.

Exeter University also set up a wholly-owned company some years ago to offer a wide range of scientific, technical and management consultancy assistance to small firms. The university reckons it probably has under one roof expertise in eighty per cent of the specialist areas a modern technologically-oriented company needs.

'We have national and international experts in some fields. They are all doing ongoing research,' pointed out Mrs Pamela Smith, the company's manager. 'They travel a lot. They get knowledge from other parts of the world and they pool their knowledge.'

Exeter University has even managed to get its students involved in the programme. 'When a firm puts a member of staff on a new project, it is likely to cost it £10,000 to £12,000 a year without being sure of the outcome. A student who's working in that area and would be interested in doing it as a project, will have academics overseeing what he does,' explained Mrs Smith.

Both sides gain. The student furthers his knowledge from first-hand experience of a real project. The company is given access to the considerable resources available at a major university, often at a cost far below that charged by private consulting groups.

As far as Exeter University is concerned, a major motivation is the fact that 'university departments, particularly science departments have got to get closer to industry and commerce'.

While many established small business entrepreneurs are shy of modern technology, a lot of start-up entrepreneurs attempt to build their companies around innovative ideas they believe can be turned into going concerns.

The Council for Small Industries in Rural Areas (CoSIRA) gives encouragement to these enterprising entrepreneurs. At its headquarters in Salisbury it has established a project workshop where prototypes of new inventions can be made up and tested to see if they are practical.

In addition, several of CoSIRA's regional offices have set up innovation centres which act as marriage bureaux bringing together bright inventors with investors who may be interested in backing a promising new idea. One such centre at Taunton has vetted hundreds of inventions, about ten per cent of which have any commercial merit.

A lot of the inventions brought to CoSIRA are weird and wonderful ideas that are never likely to be turned into practical applications. 'We've had three perpetual motion machines,' said David Patten, an organiser at CoSIRA's Taunton office. 'The irony is that the inventors don't realize they are perpetual motion machines.

'Around eighty per cent of the inventions brought to us have already been thought of before. The inventors don't realize it, but we know because we see so many products and visit so many firms in the normal course of our work.'

A panel consisting of a patent agent, an engineer and a financial specialist meet regularly to discuss the commercial potential of submitted inventions. CoSIRA helps the most promising inventors by advising them on patenting, financing and marketing.

[131]

CoSIRA makes no charge for the initial advice to inventors. If a prototype is needed involving engineering work, the inventor is asked to pay towards the costs. Patent fees and the full costs of employing a patent agent are the responsibility of the inventor.

CoSIRA Taunton holds an exhibition every year of some of the best inventions it has helped to launch. It invites leading figures, like Arthur C. Clarke, the famous author and futurologist, to open the exhibitions.

Within a very limited budget, CoSIRA Taunton also makes awards to innovative firms. David Patten would like to see a lot more support for inventive entrepreneurs, however. He considers the amount of government backing for innovation as abysmal. The Japanese government, he points out, has set up 185 innovation centres where promising inventors can go and try out their ideas. By contrast, the Taunton centre gets no government support. 'Our centre has no hardware. In essence, it is no more than a package of advice,' laments Patten.

The general lack of encouragement for scientific and technological entrepreneurs in Britain has led to a brain drain that has siphoned off many of the country's most creative minds to more accommodating places like the United States.

In the North West of Britain there is a novel experiment that is trying to reverse this unfortunate trend. It is called the Genesis Centre. From the outside, there is little to distinguish the gleaming glass and steel building with the red pillar box entrance from all the other modern complexes that stud the Birchwood Science Park at Warrington, proclaiming with bold brash architecture the new era of high-technology.

Inside the Genesis Centre, however, is to be found what must be one of the greatest concentrations of industrial scientific endeavour in the country in a veritable honeycomb of offices and laboratories.

[132]

There are computer whizz-kids poring over software simulations that measure the likely impact of an earthquake on a nuclear reactor. Down the corridor, in another anonymous laboratory, bacteriologists are examining water samples in the fight to stamp out Legionnaire's disease. In another corner of the complex, grown men toy with miniature robots used to take the slog out of chemical analysis.

As you climb the twisting staircase that leads to a seemingly endless warren of small firms with intriguing names like Impell, Varian, Phoenix and Zymark, you are likely to brush shoulders with nuclear trouble-shooters, bio-technologists, microbiologists and experts in non-destructive testing.

When it drew up its battle plans to fight chronic unemployment in its corner of the North West, Warrington & Runcorn Development Corp. saw the need for a science park similar to those that had given birth to the sunrise industries in America's technological reawakening. The Warrington planners were shrewd enough to realize, however, that there were dozens of entrepreneurial scientists with limited capital resources yearning to turn a bright idea into a flourishing business without the horrendous expense of moving into grandiose accommodation and taking on exorbitant overheads.

The Genesis Centre was conceived as a spawning ground for creative boffins, offering modest accommodation at cheap rents to give innovative ideas a chance to ferment. The key to the whole exercise was flexibility. An entrepreneur can set up at the Genesis Centre with next to no capital simply by hiring a room and a desk.

Most usually start with a 500 sq ft unit with the prospect of steadily graduating to larger accommodation of up to 5,000 sq ft as business blossoms. Several firms have grown so rapidly they have had to move to more extensive accommodation on other sites.

One micro-computer company, for example, that started

[133]

off in one of the smallest units as a one-man band ended up occupying 45,000 sq ft of its own premises and being floated on the Unlisted Securities Market.

It is not simply the flexibility it provides that has caused scientific entrepreneurs to flock to the Genesis Centre like moths to a candle. John Pownall, a director of Altwell, the company that performs microbiological testing and is involved in tracing the causes of Legionnaire's disease, admits it was the reflected image of the science park that lured him and his two fellow directors.

Before deciding on Warrington, Atwell's directors received enticing offers from other industrial developers of rent-free accommodation, but they realized that as a small new company, with no track record to speak of, they had a credibility problem. 'We had to approach large companies with household names as an unheard of little business,' Pownall recalled. 'We needed an image. If we had gone to some of these other industrial sites, which were a lot cheaper, we could have been next door to somebody fixing exhaust units or someone doing wrought-iron work. No disrespect to those companies, but we needed to be in a scientific environment.'

Several of the firms at the Genesis Centre are the offspring of US parents. They represent the second prong of the Development Corp's strategy. The American subsidiaries provide a kind of brain drain in reverse. The US parent groups, looking for a toe-hold in the British market, in a field well-established at their home base, are attracted by the concentration of high technology at Warrington and the scientific climate that has been generated.

Advanced technology is transferred across the Atlantic, British boffins with entrepreneurial flair are given their head and hundreds of jobs are created into the bargain. The Development Corp. gets the best of all worlds. It keeps highly skilled scientists in the North West, creates real jobs with a long-term future and earns good revenues from the rentals it charges.

Generally speaking, inventors often make poor entrepreneurs because they tend to become obsessed by their inventions and neglect marketing and financial control. Richard Mozley, a former mining engineer, who set up a company based on an advanced kind of hydrocylone, used to separate solids from liquids in the mineral and chemical processing industries, was careful not to fall into this trap.

He sought financial backing from the government-run National Research and Development Corporation (now the British Technology Group) to develop his invention and to produce potentially marketable prototypes. The £50,000 he received from the NRDC gave him two years' breathing space to carry out research without the pressure of running up business overheads.

In return for financial support, Mozley handed over the patent rights to his invention to NRDC. When he started to receive positive feedback from the market place, however, he formed a company and sold the hydrocyclones by paying royalties to NRDC on his own invention.

The result of this somewhat tortuous route to the market place was that Mozley was able to build a company that became highly profitable, with forty per cent annual growth rates and providing employment for twelve people. Operating at first from his home to keep overheads low, Mozley was eventually able to buy a £250,000 office and laboratory complex to run the company from.

Richard Mozley had always had an inventive mind and he first had the idea of designing an advanced hydrocyclone while doing research into mineral recovery techniques at Bristol University in the late 1960s. 'I bought one of the commercially available hydrocyclones and felt it was dreadfully designed,' recalled Mozley. 'I felt there was a need for one that not only worked well, but was easy to operate and simple to install and control.'

It was to be some years before Mozley's ideas could be put

to the test, however. In 1971, he joined a small tin processing company and eventually became a director. He later fell out with his fellow directors and left the company. 'I thought very hard about what to do and realized that the thing I enjoyed doing most and which was central to my life was invention,' said Mozley.

He had already developed good relations with NRDC and submitted two inventions for which he sought financial backing. He was given the go-ahead for both ideas, one of which was the hydrocyclone.

Shortly after starting on the projects he broke a leg. It might have seemed an ominous sign to some, but Mozley considered it a piece of good fortune. The 'enforced idleness' meant that he was obliged to manage the project, supervising his two assistants, rather than doing all the research work himself. Like most inventors, he had always been very much a 'hands-on' manager before. 'It meant I had to adopt a very different approach to these projects,' admitted Mozley.

The ability to stand back and manage the business from a distance was later to become a way of life for Mozley. After establishing his company, he spent a great deal of time travelling all over the world doing consulting work and promoting his products, confident that his staff would run day-to-day operations efficiently in his absence. As a result, the company eventually derived half its turnover from overseas orders.

The first indications that he had a market winner came from feedback from the home market, however. When Mozley became confident enough to form a company, he did not feel any resentment at having to pay NRDC royalties on his own invention. 'They put up the upfront money and they expect a return on that,' he rationalized. 'After all, some of the royalty actually comes back to me as the inventor. It's complicated but it never bothers me. Our policy is never to be afraid of paying royalties, because they are paid out of profits and you have to recognize that industrial development costs quite a lot of money.'

For a year after completing the research projects, Mozley set up as a consultant to raise capital to launch his company. He eventually established the company on £60,000 raised from bank loans and shares issued to members of his family. He was immediately faced with the problem of generating additional financial resources to develop the company's product range. He had no intention of remaining a very small company. 'If you continue as a small company you are bound to fail in the end,' he argued. 'A company has to generate quite large resources, not only to increase its product range, but to afford the customer service that is required in this day and age.'

Mozley developed the business by rapidly expanding his markets both geographically and in the range of industries he served. He diversified out of complete dependence on mineral processing industries and broadened his base. One of his major orders in the early days, for example, came from a system that recovered starch from effluent in a potato crisp factory.

He later secured a £250,000 order from the phosphate industry in Senegal, which involved 1,000 hydrocyclones.

Mozley was careful to plough most of the company's earnings back into the business 'at the expense of the balance sheet', something that tends to make bank managers nervous. But he felt the company's ultimate success more than justified the strategy.

Getting in on the ground floor of a new industrial technology can offer rich rewards for a small indepenent company, but it also carries considerable risks. For Y & S Electrics, a company that helped to pioneer the development of automated industrial control systems, the experience of crossing new frontiers was both enlightening and chastening.

The company's pre-eminence in a young industry gained it

[137]

entrée to some major blue chip customers, including Ford Motor Co., BAT, the British Steel Corp. and Pirelli. With limited financial resources, however, it had to tread carefully in ensuring that it could meet the high expectations of such major groups and still remain profitable.

The introduction of microprocessors to industrial control systems is a relatively recent development and has only lately become the established way to control automation. 'Obviously, there's a certain amount of risk attached to that – not only making sure that you get things right, but also in the way that one looks at it commercially,' explained Trevis Chiles, the firm's managing director. 'You are very much in the realms of the unknown. You have a fairly clear idea of what you want to do and how you are going to achieve it, but there are hidden snags you aren't aware of.

'We've learned an awful lot of lessons, particularly relating to specifications where we had to be a hundred per cent clear on the client's requirements. Because the client is often not very familiar with microprocessor systems, he is looking to you for guidance. At times, the client's interpretation of what his requirements are have been different to ours.'

Chiles admitted that before he had learned better the company was sometimes over-optimistic about what it could achieve and a little naive in its commercial approach. 'Even though this business looks very glamorous from the outside, it hasn't returned the sort of profits we would have liked to have seen,' he said.

Y & S was set up in 1973 by Chiles and another director, both electrical engineers who had been working as draughtsmen for Westland, the helicopter company. They left Westland with little cash, but considerable enthusiasm.

Recalled Chiles: 'We were at the age when you ignore the risks and go for the challenge.' To build up capital for their fledgling firm, the two men originally offered their services as electrical engineers, carrying out sub-contract work.

Their first breakthrough came when they secured a contract to design a system for controlling the mechanical handling of pistons for the Sierra motorcar at Ford's Dagenham plant. After two years, Y & S had generated enough business designing industrial control systems to be able to set up their company in earnest.

Soon afterwards, two major contracts came their way. One was to remodel the control system for the assembly of up-and-over garage doors manufactured by a subsidiary of Westland. It was the first introduction of microprocessing into the automation business in Britain and provided Y & S with valuable experience. The second opportunity, worth £100,000, involved a control system for a Ford manufacturing plant.

When Andrew Greenslade decided to set up a company based on laser technology, he too found himself in the forefront of industrial developments, which offered both opportunities and high risks. His main problem was the large amount of capital required.

Although laser systems don't cost a great deal to run, the initial outlay is quite high. Greenslade's system, which he built himself around a modern Ferranti laser, cost in the region of £150,000, far more money than he could raise personally.

He investigated the various government grants available and where he needed to be located to take best advantage of them. 'With a laser company there is no natural geographical location,' he pointed out. 'Therefore, we looked at the grant areas available to us. Being a high-tech, high capital cost operation, we wanted to get the maximum amount of assistance we could.'

He finally settled on the West Country, where he was able to obtain regional selective assistance and a regional development grant, totalling £36,000, towards the start-up costs. In addition, he raised £90,000 from NatWest under the government guaranteed loan scheme and chipped in £50,000 of his own capital.

Greenslade claims to have operated Britain's first commercial laser back in the early 1970s when the technology was in its infancy. He gave Ferranti, this country's leading manufacturer of industrial lasers, the chance to test the process in an actual working environment. The later, more sophisticated lasers developed by Ferranti owe a considerable amount to the experiments which were conducted in the workshops of Greenslade's former company in the North of England.

When Greenslade came to set up his latest company, he had to choose carefully the industrial applications he should go for. Even though lasers are highly versatile in terms of what they can cut, largely because they never actually make contact with the surface of the material, they also have their limitations. 'We fit between the one-off and the multi-thousand runs, where conventional productions methods are more appropriate,' explained Greenslade. 'When you are talking about mass production markets, such as the motor industry, lasers are unsuitable.'

On the other hand, lasers come into their own when it comes to cutting out intricate patterns from metals, such as when producing a complex template for checking castings in a Rolls-Royce diesel engine.

When a company taking part in an international welding exhibition needed an elaborate map of the world cut out of stainless steel to use as a backdrop for its stand, it turned to Greenslade's company. 'That's a prime example of what a laser can do,' said Greenslade. Its fast and highly accurate cutting power is equally appropriate for carving up the parts for heavy armoured vehicles or, at the other end of the scale, in the manufacture of small washers and electronic components.

One of the fastest growing technologies in Britain is the technique of giving 'vision' to machines. Clearly, if robots can be given the ability to 'see', there will be very few tasks they won't be able to do which are now done by man. Bill Adaway, one of the country's leading experts in this area, fervently believes automation is the key to survival for British manufacturing industries, which are increasingly under threat from low-cost goods imported from abroad.

Adaway contends that any manufacturing company not already installing or planning to install machines to improve productivity is one with no realistic commercial future. He also sees automation as a vital aid to quality control. In addition, he sees automation freeing human operators from tedious, repetitive and possibly dangerous tasks, enabling them to concentrate on jobs requiring knowledge and experience.

Adaway is proving that small technologically-oriented firms can be run within reasonable cost parameters by the way he operates his own company, Computer Recognition Systems Ltd (CRS). He has seen too many firms collapse as a result of technologically-obsessed entrepreneurs allowing their creativity to outstrip their grip on reality to allow the same to happen to him.

'I have no intention whatever of allowing this company to fail,' he declared. He intends to survive by gearing his company to markets that minimize risk and ensure that he lives within his financial resources. He calls the technique 'comb marketing'.

'I've spent a lot of effort in planning which markets to approach, seeking out markets of exactly the right size,' said Adaway.

By combing the market, CRS has gone for a large number of widely diverse markets, which call for batches of no more than between ten to fifty of a particular 'vision' product. It means it is spreading its options among a whole range of markets that the major companies are unlikely to be interested in because of their limited size.

'In that environment, you can build yourself a very stable business,' pointed out Adaway. 'If you've got a lot of those markets, as we have, you must be fairly safe, because there is no way any one company is going to come along and wipe them all out because they're all different. The technical skill of being able to do that is to develop a range of products which lets you serve all of those different markets without having a vast R&D overhead. We've achieved that by the particular modular architecture that we've chosen, designed specifically for this comb marketing approach.'

CRS's approach has been to look into its crystal ball and try to predict the upcoming markets where machine vision is likely to be in demand. It then developed hardware that is likely to fit into that new requirement. It has built up a range of around sixty separate pieces of hardware, which it can 'mix and match' to meet market requirements.

Machine vision now embraces an enormous variety of applications, ranging from high-speed number plate recognition of cars racing down a motorway, to face and finger print recognition, fruit grading, industrial robot guidance, military target tracking and print quality inspection. 'All these things, in vastly different industries, are actually done with the same pieces of equipment, configured in a different way, because of the modular approach we've managed to take.'

Adaway contrasts his 'comb marketing' technique with the 'Big Bang' approach that tends to be adopted in the United States. 'A lot of American vision companies perceived that there is a market in machine vision. They read a market forecast that says this is going to be a billion dollar industry by 1990, which may or may not be true,' he said. 'They raise a million dollars, go to the local university and ask what it has got that they can make. Then all the money is blown away on advertising, marketing and salesmen rushing around in estate cars.

'If the market suddenly goes well, they'll make millions, but if it doesn't grow, they plummet like a stone. Actually a lot of them are going broke now.'

CRS's approach has been much more cautious. 'We're gearing our expenditure to the size the market is becoming. We are trying to pick these niche markets to protect ourselves. If there should be an explosive growth in the market, IBM might come in and sell millions of vision systems, but they still won't be able to touch our comb markets because they're only modest in size. It's all geared to survival.'

Case Study A

The Upward Spiral

After working for several years in his father's traditional blacksmith's business, Michael Jordan decided to go back to college and take a diploma in business studies. He chose as the theme of his final thesis the setting up of a hypothetical spiral staircase company. The examining board at the college was so impressed with the detailed research that had gone into the project that they thought it must have been based on a real company.

As soon as he had obtained his diploma, Jordan did, in fact, turn theory into reality. He walked away from college with a blueprint for a company that was later to make spiral staircases for some of the world's most prestigious buildings.

Jordan's eye for good design developed while working for his father, one of the top craftsmen in the country, who placed exacting demands on those he employed. To prove their worth, Michael Jordan and his brother Roger spent 400 hours making an intricate dragon lantern. It was based on one Jordan's father had designed for the baronial home of the Duke of Northumberland, and it won first prize in a national blacksmith contest.

But Jordan could see a dwindling market for the traditional blacksmith's craftwork and he felt he needed to channel the age-old skills into a product for the twentieth century. At the time he went back to college to study management, his father's blacksmith business was developing iron-work designs for a royal palace in Jeddah. The project incorporated several staircases and Jordan used them as the launch-pad for a six-month study on setting up a design and manufacturing firm.

As part of the research, Jordan investigated the competition. 'The astonishing thing was that there were only six or seven people nationally doing staircases. So there was a great big void for someone to step into,' he recalled.

A total of eight staircases was required for the Jeddah project. Jordan's first thought was to contract out all but the wrought-iron balustrade work, but he soon concluded that the staircases produced by other firms did not match the quality of the local craftsmanship. It became patently obvious that he would ultimately have to make complete staircases himself.

'At this point we had to think fairly hard about the financial implications,' recalled Jordan, who launched his company from a portable workshop adjoining his father's forge, but later moved into a large unit on a local industrial estate. 'We started the company with an investment of £4,000 which was minimal.'

Initially, Jordan built up the company's financial resources largely with earnings from design contracts. When it came to manufacturing, he decided from the outset he would need to construct staircases from a material that matched the elegance of the ironwork. He developed a process for creating concrete structures that closely resembled sculptured marble.

A stand at the Ideal Home Exhibition shortly after the company was set up, attracted the attention of wealthy Arabs, who placed contracts which opened up the Middle East market for the small firm almost before it had got off the ground.

It soon became apparent to Jordan that he needed a computer-aided design system to reduce the amount of time-consuming manual work being carried out by his draughtsmen. The fees being charged by the consultants Jordan approached were more than his small company could afford. So he sought the help of a local technical college. The students were only too delighted to be given a real-life project to tackle and came up with a system tailor-made to the staircase firm's needs. Jordan was presented with a facility that could display different design configurations at the touch of a button. His customers could be shown computer graphic variations to standard staircase models in a matter of seconds, leaving the firm's draughtsmen free to spend their time on more creative pursuits.

Case Study B

A Measured Approach to Technology

One of the favoured routes to starting up a new business based on advanced technology is first to take on a distributorship to build up a solid financial base before taking the plunge into manufacturing. Dave Davies, a former commercial manager for a leading electronics firm, took just such a cautious approach in establishing a company called Measurement Systems, which eventually achieved a turnover of several million pounds.

While working for his former company, Davies became aware that the application of computers to measurement systems was a growing market with enormous potential. 'The trend was towards microprocessors and lower cost systems giving much better price performance,' recalled Davies. Unable to convince his former company that this was the best route to follow, Davies eventually left to pursue the idea himself.

To reduce the risks and the heavy financial outlay involved in developing the product ideas he had in mind, Davies took on the UK distributorship for a single-board computer made by Rockwell, the major US group. With gross margins of thirty-five per cent on the products it distributed for Rockwell and another US manufacturer, Davies' firm made a small paper profit in its first year, but this was wiped out by the £20,000 development costs needed to produce a measurement product to sit on the back of the Rockwell computer. Davies, in fact, ended the first year £50,000 in the red. But the following year he managed to obtain a £20,000 development grant from the Department of Industry and managed to make enough to cancel out the previous year's losses.

Davies was now poised to go from strength to strength, but he had a difficult decision to make. The distribution business offered good potential for profitable growth, but he hadn't lost sight of his original goal – to make his own products for a market he was convinced was going to expand exponentially. The trouble was he had insufficient financial resources to keep both operations going. One had to be sacrificed and after a great deal of agonizing, he opted to abandon the proven distributorship for the unproven manufacturing operation.

'It was a painful decision to make,' admitted Davies. 'We had managed to take the distributorship to £500,000 a year and there was definitely £200,000 worth of gross margin there for very little effort. But we just didn't have the cash to support both operations – and the banks simply didn't want to know. So Measurement Systems was literally started from scratch again in 1984 when we switched entirely to making our own products. We put an enormous amount of energy and enthusiasm into the early stages – a phenomenal amount of man hours.'

To succeed, Davies knew that he had to keep his feet firmly on the ground and not get carried away by inventive flair. He drew up the product specifications in broad outline, but left the detailed design to an outside consultant.

One thing he regarded as essential was a good in-house sales force that would spend time with prospective customers understanding their requirements. 'At the end of the day a business is all about customers,' declared Davies, 'a lot of companies lose sight of that fact.'

Taking this as his credo, Davies drew on his experience as a former commercial manager to put together the finest sales force he could muster. He left the salesmen in no doubt that Measurement Systems was to be a market-driven operation. 'Our overall selling approach is market oriented, not the traditional selling approach,' explained Davies. 'We built our business from the customer upwards, rather than from market forecasts. We set targets on our customers. We say, that company could potentially spend this amount this year and this is how we have got to achieve it.'

As part of this market-oriented strategy, Davies has tried to make the firm's measurement systems simple and easy to operate. 'The first thing we do is address the user with something he can understand,' he said. 'One of the problems with the electronics market is that it tends to be very incestuous. We love to sell each other super-duper products, but the real growth market is the people who don't really understand electronics and are frightened of it. We try to understand the customer's business first, so that when he sees a product he isn't frightened. He sees something he recognizes.'

Recognizing the limitations of a fledgling firm, Davies was not over-ambitious in going after the dozens of markets that were opening up in the electronic measuring field. He targeted five major areas – management information systems (MIS) and the petrochemical, steel, motorcar and aerospace industries. At the same time, he designed his products in a modular fashion to give the company the flexibility of being able to move rapidly into new market niches when enticing opportunities arose.

Davies was convinced that the potentially most exciting market was MIS. He developed real-time information systems for monitoring automatic production lines in conjunction with companies like Unilever, BAT, Thorn EMI and Coca-Cola. In one case, Measurement Systems came up with a £3,000 software package which replaced a system a company was developing at a cost of £70,000.

Davies was driven by a conviction that improving the performance of production lines was one of the few remaining areas where British industry can reduce its costs dramatically. 'When you think about it, there is little more that can be done to reduce the price of a cigarette or a bar of soap,' he rationalized, 'the real gains are to be made from real-time monitoring of production lines. The performance benefits are absolutely astronomical. A five per cent improvement in the performance of companies processing £400 million a year means £20 million goes straight to the bottom line.'

With the evidence of such rapid growth, Measurement Systems soon overcame the problem it had experienced in the early days of raising extra cash. Offers came from three venture capital groups for secondary financing. The company opted for a package put up by CIN Industrial Investments, the venture capital arm of the British Coal Pension Funds. CIN injected £300,000 into Measurement Systems for convertible and non-convertible preference shares.

Under a 'ratchet' agreement with Measurement Systems, CIN reserved the right to convert £200,000 of the injection into a ten per cent shareholding provided the company met pre-defined business goals. If it failed to meet the business goals, CIN would claim fourteen per cent of the shares.

Turning an Invention into a Company

It is not difficult to think of a new product idea. It is much harder to transform the invention into something practical that will sell viably in the market place, as many entrepreneurs have found to their cost. The Council for Small Industries in Rural Areas has drawn up a useful set of guidelines for creative entrepreneurs:

- *Is it original*? There is little point in inventing a product that has already been developed. Your first task must be to research 'prior art'. This can be done by reference to the trade press, reference libraries or by consulting a patent agent. Patent agents have a remarkably wide knowledge of inventions and industrial processes, and patent abridgements are kept at the Science Reference Library in London and a few regional libraries, such as Bristol Central.
- *Is there a market*? An important early decision should be is there a market for my product? Try to evaluate competing products. Consider their strengths and weaknesses.

  Are the advantages of your product sufficient to sell it? Would a manufacturer change his production line and re-tool to make your invention?

  Is the market sector for which you are aiming increasing or decreasing? Is it fashionable? Seasonal? To whom will it appeal? Who are your potential buyers?

[148]

- *What protection does the invention merit?* If your market research reinforces the originality of the invention then protection by patents or other means should be considered.

  A patent by itself will not make you a fortune. Initially, you may have to disburse considerable cash. You will be wise to engage the services of a chartered patent agent for his breadth of technical knowledge and legal drafting skills. The initial filing of a United Kingdom patent application could cost between £400 and £700.

There is a school of thought that says you should get on with the development and exploitation of the invention rather than be concerned with patenting. But if you neglect patent action at the start, you will almost inevitably lose all legal redress against unauthorized copying.

You do not have to incur the full cost of a formal application in the first instance. Most patent agents will advise on lodging an initial application to avoid the worst pitfalls. This will give you up to twelve months in which to develop an idea further and to see whether it is likely to be worth seeking full patent protection and incurring the subsequent costs of piloting it through official procedures up to grant of a patent.

Ideas themselves are not patentable. To be patentable, an invention must be capable of industrial application (including agriculture). Artistic works, computer programs, mathematical theories or business schemes are outside the scope of patent law.

A United Kingdom patent gives protection to inventions produced in this country. Infringements will occur if any foreign made replica is sold or used here. Various foreign treaties are now in force to gain world protection, but in the main foreign patenting is horrendously complicated and expensive.

Apart from patenting, protection through copyright might

be gained by registering the design under the Registered Designs Act 1949. Many products rely to a large extent on their commercial prosperity by exterior novelty and recognition. Examples are the Coca-Cola bottle and the Marmite jar. Design registration covers features which appeal solely to the eye. They will not protect mechanical ingenuity.

Design registrations tend to be applied to textiles, wallpaper, jewellery and domestic products.

Trade marks are a most valuable method of promoting a good product. The rights to use 'Kodak' or 'Hoover' are worth millions. Unlike patents and registered designs, trade marks registration can be accepted after production of the goods. The costs are low and the mark can be maintained indefinitely.

Few inventors combine ingenuity, financial muscle and the management ability to produce a complete manufactured product. Successful ideas take off because of a marriage between the innovator and a manufacturer with enough vision, courage and patience to pursue the idea.

Approaches should be made to manufacturers of similar products. These names can be readily found in trade year books and association or industrial directories, such as Kompass.

Confidentiality can be a difficult hurdle. Some companies may say that they cannot accept inventions submitted in confidence. If their own R&D department is working on the same idea, they would not wish to disclose that fact. If they later launch a similar product, they could be subjected to accusations of piracy.

If your invention has commercial potential, you as patent holder can license the rights to manufacture. Depending on your skills as a negotiator and cash requirements, you can either sell the licence outright for a once-and-for-all payment or insist on a down payment with successive royalties on sales expressed as a percentage per unit. If you enter into an exclusive licence, ensure you obtain a get-out clause if nothing is developed.

A comprehensive range of booklets on the subject can be obtained from The Chartered Institute of Patent Agents, Staple Inn Buildings, High Holborn, London WC1V 7PZ. (Tel. 01–405 9450).

7

THE SMOTHERED
ENTREPRENEUR

Getting to Grips with Red Tape

IF small business entrepreneurs have been shy of new manufacturing techniques, they have rushed to embrace the
technological revolution that micro-computers promised to
bring to administration. In many cases they have burned their
fingers.

When the micro-computer revolution took the business
world by storm, promising to make a dramatic impact on the
way companies are run, manufacturers were not geared to
cope with the runaway boom that ensued. The answer
seemed to be to distribute through dealers.

But in their haste to climb on the bandwagon, many manufacturers appointed dealers who had little knowledge of what
desk-top micro-computers are capable of doing or of the way
companies operate.

The result was that a lot of businesses, lured by the magic of
the micros, ended up buying machines that they were not
trained to handle. As a consequence, many of these sparkling
new computers, which offered so much promise, ended up
gathering dust in dark corners of offices, abandoned by businessmen who had lost patience in trying to make them work

or who lacked the time to read complicated manuals.

While this was a headache for the businessmen left grappling with ineffective systems, it presented a golden opportunity for computer experts with entrepreneurial flair. Computer service bureaux began cropping up all over Britain. They were run by professionals experienced in the finer points of operating computers and who took the time to understand businessmen's problems in order to supply the most appropriate equipment to meet specific needs.

One such company was set up by Michael Meredith and his wife Susan. Meredith has more than fifteen years' experience of the computer industry behind him, during which he has seen it pass through a series of evolutionary developments, from the big mainframe computers to mini computers and finally the micro.

During market research, Meredith came across many businessmen who despaired of making their micro-computers work effectively.

'If you're running a business of your own, you can't afford the time to research how to put your sales ledger up on the machine, what sort of reports you want to come out of it, what sort of coding structure you've got to install, whether you should buy this package or that to suit your specific needs,' he comments.

'The retail outlets are not set up to offer the kinds of support the businessman needs. They are basically set up to sell boxes and you go away and do your own thing. If the manual is gibberish, you shouldn't have bought the package. We have aimed to bring a degree of professionalism into the affair.'

Alec Ovens became so concerned about the widespread ignorance displayed by small businessmen when it came to computer technology that he switched the main thrust of his company from selling hardware to offering advice. Previously, he had run a dealership for a leading computer manufacturer. But he saw a more urgent demand for his experience in advising small businessmen about how to seek out the system that best fitted their needs.

'I find it very strange that some businessmen allow logic to fly out of the window when it comes to buying computer systems,' reflects Ovens. 'I know companies that have bought computer systems that have never been used. Businessmen seem to get carried away when buying computers. I don't know whether it's the pressure of computer salesmen or whether the businessmen, who are often quite senior people, are afraid of admitting their ignorance.'

Ovens concluded that there was nobody small businesses could turn to for unprejudiced advice. Practically everyone they were likely to approach were representing one or more computer manufacturer. He regarded it as unreasonable to be both a computer salesmen and someone claiming to offer unbiased advice. So he turned his company into an advisory and training operation.

'It's very difficult to find an unbiased source of advice in the computer field,' contends Ovens. 'The most likely place a businessman would go would be to his accountant. But the reality is that in the same way accountants were agents for insurance companies in the past, the professional bodies have now accepted a commission arrangement with the suppliers of computer systems, so long as they disclose to the client that this is the case.'

Some accountancy groups are, however, offering a way out of the dilemma by providing a service that takes over the financial administrative chores for small businessmen. The Profit Centre is one such computerized book-keeping service run by professional accountants. The service collates small firms' trading figures on a regular basis and issues early warnings when a company appears to be financially off course.

'Small businessmen tend to get swallowed up by marketing, production, personnel, all that kind of thing,' says

Brian Payne, a director of The Profit Centre. 'They lose sight of financial control. Over the past few years, however, there has been mounting pressure from the banks who are putting up money to have regular financial information.

'They might start by asking for an interim half-yearly review of what's going on and then step it up to a quarterly review in a well-borrowed situation. If, every time that is required, it involves picking up a brown paper bag full of books and starting from scratch, it becomes a very expensive and time-consuming exercise.'

Payne points out that the technology is available today to release businessmen from such time-consuming chores, but if they don't understand properly how to operate micro-computers it will only add to their burdens. An increasing number of them are opting to hand the problem over to skilled professionals who are familiar with the technology and are experts in accountancy procedures.

'In my estimation, they could give micro-computers away free with cornflakes, but ninety per cent of the businessmen using them would still run into problems because of the lack of background knowledge of the accountancy issues within the program,' suggests Payne.

'It makes far more sense to use a central point of technology and accountancy expertise which simply processes the information on behalf of the businessman. Computer bureaux or firms of accountants have worked on that basis for some time, but we thought we could add an extra dimension by greatly simplifying the records that small businessmen have to keep.'

The Profit Centre has developed a system of feeding the computer directly from the businessman's cheque book paying-in slips, using computer code numbers to denote the nature of the transaction. This practically abolishes the need for normal book-keeping. The businessmen are supplied with computer print-outs at regular intervals, giving them updates on their financial affairs according to a pre-determined format.

'We are able to set up a regular accounting format for a particular client to whatever specification he requires. It is infinitely adaptable,' explains Payne. 'We tend to work off about a dozen basic models of particular businesses. We sit down with a particular small businessman, show him our version of a similar business – what expense and income headings we would expect to see. But he can then ask to shuffle that around to give him any depth of analysis he wants on his figures. He can, for example, break his sales up into a hundred different product lines.'

The businessman gets a regular print-out of his financial data at whatever frequency he chooses, normally every quarter, for which he pays a small basic monthly charge. There is no set-up charge or hidden extras, unless the business is particularly complicated in its structure, involving sophisticated management accountancy requirements. In this case, The Profit Centre makes a charge for the time involved in sitting down with the businessman to analyse his particular requirements.

In the main, The Profit Centre leaves it to the businessman's own accountant or financial adviser to interpret the figures on the print-out. To a limited extent the service acts as an early warning system: 'The whole system is designed to highlight actual performance on a regular basis against budgeted performance and indeed against prior years' performance where that is appropriate. It is designed to highlight any point where the results are going adrift from plan and we are in a position to advise on making that plan,' says Payne.

The service does, however, stop short of giving taxation advice, for example, because it is felt that should be the role of the client firm's professional adviser.

Payne points out that the real advantage of the service is

[157]

that it constantly updates the financial data and the information is always complete, something that helps to keep businessmen on the good side of their bank manager. 'The principal criticism in the Robson Rhodes Report on the small firms Loan Guarantee Scheme was the absence of regular financial minotoring,' notes Payne. 'Regular financial monitoring can be a very expensive and time-consuming exercise for a small business unless there's an off-the-shelf service to provide it.'

The same could be said of all the other administrative chores the small businessman has to grapple with. There is no question that he needs all the assistance he can find to cope with them. Red tape and government bureaucracy consistently come out top of the list in numerous surveys conducted among small businessmen. They often complain that they have to undertake the same onerous amount of red tape as large corporations with far greater resources in order to comply with government regulations.

Attempts have been made by the government in recent years to reduce the red tape burden on small businessmen so that they can be freed to get on with the serious task of building up their companies and creating jobs. But few, if any, businessmen feel that the government has gone anywhere near far enough in this direction.

The Forum of Private Industry, which lobbies the government on behalf of small businesses, has calculated that an entrepreneur planning to set up a small limited company would need to spend a solid twenty-four hours ploughing through all the legislation involved in VAT, PAYE, National Insurance, Health and Safety at Work and Employment law. He would have to read and understand a total of 269,000 words in no less than 27 booklets and pamphlets.

In addition, The Forum estimated the entrepreneur has to spend ten hours a week complying with government regulations at an average cost of £2,000 a year. The penalties for failing to do so can amount to fines of up to £9,000 and up to two years' imprisonment.

Stan Mendham, The Forum's founder, has identified thirty-one different forms or regulations that have to be dealt with or provided when a business takes on a single employee. He has also counted up thirty-four clerical operations involved in calculating the net pay for each employee. 'In the light of this burden of government regulations and the fear of getting it wrong, it is not surprising that small businesses are not prepared to make their businesses grow and hence employ people,' says Mendham.

One of the most onerous burdens the small business has to tolerate is VAT, which it collects on behalf of the government. Before new measures were introduced by the Chancellor in the 1987 Budget, VAT often had to be paid to Customs and Excise prior to the businessman receiving it from his customers, a situation that was exacerbated by the widespread practice of delaying payment of due invoices. In one infamous example, a company was obliged to make out a cheque to the Vatman for £30,000 when only £5,000 of it had actually been received from its customers.

This scandalous state of affairs was tackled in the 1987 Budget when the Chancellor announced that in future all businesses with turnovers of less than £250,000 would be allowed to wait until they had received the cash from their customers before being liable for VAT. He also abolished the requirement for firms to pay VAT on a quarterly basis by making it a once-a-year payment. In addition, he increased the VAT threshold from £20,500 to £21,300 and the registration period from 10 days to 30 days.

Some lobbying groups firmly believe the VAT threshold (the turnover level at which companies become liable for VAT) should be raised considerably higher. The Forum of Private Industry, for example, argues that only a small percentage of the total VAT revenue comes from small businesses. Yet small businesses have to undertake the same time-consuming administrative chore.

It could equally be argued that the present system is not cost-effective for the government and there is every indication that the government would like to raise the threshold still further. The problem is that the Chancellor has already increased it to the maximum permissible under a Common Market agreement. Amazingly, there are several European countries which have significantly lower VAT thresholds.

The situation was made even worse for British businesses when the government recently introduced tougher penalties for failing to register for VAT on time. In the rush of running a fledgling firm, it is easy enough to overlook the requirement. Sometimes small businessmen don't even realize that they have reached the threshold until several months after the event because of slack book-keeping. Instead of treating this as a minor misdemeanour, comparable with forgetting to buy a road fund licence, Customs and Excise has been empowered by the government to exact harsh retribution in the form of heavy fines, threatening the viability of already vulnerable small firms.

The Forum of Private Industry has drawn up a set of proposals that would cut by more than half the time and costs incurred by small businesses in complying with government regulations. The Forum believes the proposals would also encourage firms to expand, coax businesses out of the 'black economy' and stimulate the formation of new companies.

The crux of the proposals is a single standard form produced by each government department for use by small businesses. Each form would satisfy all of the duties and responsibilities of small firms for that department. The Forum also advocated that small businesses should be made a special case as far as government regulations are concerned and that small limited liability companies should operate as a special legal entity designated as MLC (Micro Limited Company).

The National Federation for the Self Employed and Small Businesses (NFSE), which with 50,000 members, claims to be the largest organization in Britain representing the interests of small firms, believes that the only real way to secure a better deal for small businesses is to influence legislation at the European level, where many of our commercial laws are now formulated.

The NFSE's representatives are spending an increasing amount of time in Brussels monitoring new legislation affecting small businesses. The NFSE had previously found that when the British government invited consultation on new business proposals, they were often virtually *fait accompli*. Observes Bill Oliver, chairman of the NFSE's EEC Committee: 'The trouble was we were getting to hear about things very late in the day, because government departments get to consider these things quite late on in the process. The time to be influencing proposed legislation is at the earliest stage when the committees of the European Commission are thinking about it.'

The European Commission is only obliged to consult international bodies, not national organizations. So NFSE decided to join an existing international organization representing business interests on a pan-European basis. It chose to become a member of the European Committee for Small and Medium Sized Independent Companies (Europmi), which has a number of similar national organizations to the NFSE affiliated to it from such countries as West Germany, France, Italy and Belgium.

It seems inevitable that the growing groundswell of opinion that small businesses need to be set free from tiresome regulatory burdens will eventually be heeded by government and by those with the power to influence legislation. In the meantime, the burdens continue to add to the many obstacles faced by the one-dimensional entrepreneur. Most of his problems can be reduced by his own efforts. Red tape is something that only politicians can get to grips with. But it is certain that small businessmen, through their lobbying groups, will continue to exert pressure until the just cause is won.

8

THE MATURE ENTREPRENEUR

When the Small Business Comes of Age

EVERY small business entrepreneur must find his own route to success. There is no guaranteed formula for survival and growth. One entrepreneur's reaction to a crisis will be different to another's. The chances of survival will be much greater, however, if the entrepreneur is aware of the pitfalls that lie ahead and is prepared to tackle them in a rational manner. The experience of others who have trodden the road before can at least light his way.

There are numerous questions the would-be entrepreneur needs to ask himself before setting out on that road, as this book has tried to illustrate. He must first be honest with himself about whether he is entrepreneurial material, whether he has got what it takes. He must examine his own inner resources and try to gauge whether he has the stamina, dedication and sheer bloodymindedness to keep going against all manner of adversities.

He must recognize that he is almost certainly a one-dimensional entrepreneur who excels at one particular facet of running a business, but is highly vulnerable in all the other disciplines. He must explore all the different ways to compensate for those weaknesses. In doing so, he may conclude that he does not have the right armoury for the battle that inevitably lies ahead. He may prefer the less precarious option of taking on a franchise or perhaps joining a co-operative.

If, however, he decides that he wants to become a full-blooded small business entrepreneur, he must make every effort to gather together all the considerable resources he will need to make his business idea a viable concern. Not the least of his requirements will be financial backing, either in the form of a bank loan or an equity investment, unless he is in the fortunate position of having private means. He must often be prepared to put up his private possessions, usually his family home, as collateral for a loan. This is the moment of truth. If he is prepared to gamble with his most prized possessions, the would-be entrepreneur will at least be certain that his commitment is strong. Once he has raised enough capital to get his company up and running, the financial problems will by no means be over. Getting the major order from a prestigious company may be the breakthrough the entrepreneur has been waiting for. But does he have the financial muscle to fund it? If not, can he afford to raise the extra cash? Should it be in the form of a loan or an equity investment? If the latter, how much of his company is he prepared to give up to an 'outsider'?

He may be tempted to finance his growth entirely out of profits. Some entrepreneurs are proud to boast they have done just that. But financial experts argue that new machinery and equipment should not be purchased out of working capital. If the small business is healthy, it should be able to afford the interest on a loan. But what sounds sensible in theory may be hard to put into practice in the real business world. It is often tempting to do what seems most expedient.

However much finance the entrepreneur manages to raise, it will all be water down the drain if he hasn't got his marketing right. The entrepreneur who assumes that his product will sell like hot cakes from day one without first testing customer reaction is almost certainly doomed to failure. And even if his products do sell well in this country, there is no guarantee they will find ready markets in other countries. Even if they do, the small business that gets its pricing policy wrong for export markets will experience serious problems.

At some stage, the successful small business entrepreneur will almost certainly have to consider fairly substantial investments in modern technology in order to compete with rival firms at home and abroad. He will have to judge whether his company can justify such expenditure. On the other hand, he will have to consider what sort of future lies ahead for the company if he doesn't have the courage to install modern equipment in time to keep pace with competitors.

If the small business entrepreneur has given proper consideration to all these basic rules and has enjoyed a reasonable dose of good luck (an almost essential prerequisite for success these days), he will experience the immense pleasure of having turned a nebulous idea into a flourishing concern.

Once a small business gets the formula right, the growth rate can be surprisingly rapid. Entrepreneurs who started experimenting with raw materials in a back garden shed can find themselves a few years later touring enormous factories, buzzing with activity and churning out products at a phenomenal rate.

It is sometimes hard to grasp that so much has happened so quickly. Before he knows it, the entrepreneur can wake up one morning to find that he is no longer the custodian of a small business, but the chief executive of a medium-to-large company that promises to join the ranks of the country's more successful industries. The Would-Be Entrepreneur has become a Mature Entrepreneur.

The transition often creeps up on entrepreneurs unsuspectingly and the problems it poses can be almost as threatening as the dangers that engulfed him in the early stages of setting up the company. One of the hardest things for a successful mature entrepreneur to recognise is that he cannot for ever keep control of all the aspects of running his business.

It is a natural instinct for him to try to do so. After all, he conceived the company. He was the one who nurtured it through all the growing pains. It is easy for him to be convinced that nobody else, not even his closest and most loyal employees, can understand as he does what really makes the company tick.

But the inevitable day will come when, if he fails to relinquish his all-pervasive influence soon enough, he will start to lose control. It will become physically impossible for him to keep track of all the developments taking place. There simply will not be enough hours in the day. Because, however, his employees have become accustomed to all the major decisions being channelled through the founder-entrepreneur, they will have grown up in a climate in which personal initiative has not necessarily been encouraged. It will take a clear signal from the company's owner to convince them that things have changed.

Without such a signal, employees will feel stifled. Their ability to grow with the company will become stunted. Their personal potential will either never materialise or they will simply leave to join a company where their talents will perhaps be more fully appreciated and realised. In either case, it can be a serious loss to the original business at a time when it needs the support of all its employees.

Fortunately, most entrepreneurs see the dangers in time of hanging on to absolute power too long. It may take one or two minor crises to bring it home to them, but eventually they will wake up to the realisation that their company is in a different league and requires a different style of management. It is time for autocracy to give way to professional management.

[166]

This does not imply that the company has been badly managed up to this point. Indeed, if it was not being run efficiently it would probably have never survived that long and some would argue that a good dose of autocratic management is appropriate for a small business in its early stages of development. What has basically happened is that the company's operations have grown so vast that each division, whether it be marketing, finance, production, public relations, has become a mini-business in its own right and requires to be run as such by someone who has the authority to make decisions without having to refer back to the top man all the time.

Once the founder-entrepreneur realises this, he has a crucial decision to make. Does he have the managerial talent within the company that he can rely on to share the load? Or must he go outside the company and hire 'professional' managers with a proven track record?

Making the wrong decision can be calamitous. If he demonstrates a lack of faith in his own loyal employees by recruiting outside talent, he will of course demotivate them and probably lose their goodwill, something that can have serious repercussions for the future development of the company.

If, on the other hand, he decides he has the skills within the company's own ranks and that the only way to fulfil the potential of his own team is to put it to the test, he may also be gambling with the future of the company. By the time he discovers his faith was misplaced irreparable harm may be done to a business it has taken him years to build up.

There are of course no pat answers to the dilemma. The founder-entrepreneur will have to use his own judgement. It is certainly true to say that some people never shine until they are given authority. The only way to find out if they have what it takes to succeed is to plunge them in at the deep end. The founder-entrepreneur might also be influenced in his decision by the knowledge that 'professional' managers can be an anathema to the true entrepreneur who has probably operated more by instinct than by pragmatic management. He may simply find it impossible to work with professionals and may be left with little choice but to fall back on home-grown talent, even if he has some doubts about the capabilities of those concerned.

It was just such a dilemma that faced Gerry Hazlewood, founder and chairman of Westwood Engineering. Hazlewood built the company up from nothing. He began by bending pieces of metal in a garden shed to make simple rotary mowers over eighteen years ago. Today, Westwood produces around 13,000 garden tractors a year, commands seventy per cent of the UK market and has a turnover of about £12 million.

By almost any measure the company can be counted among British industry's most outstanding success stories. But for some time Hazlewood had been experiencing nagging doubts about the way the company was being run. One morning, in a blinding flash, it suddenly clicked what the problem was. For a company of its size, employing 300 people, he was still playing too much of a 'hands-on' role in management. Because he had built Westwood from scratch, he knew every inch of it and his influence was all-pervasive. Inevitably, he was cramping everybody else's style. In addition, he was trying to handle more jobs than it was physically possible to cope with.

As a result, there were signs that some areas of the company were becoming neglected. In trying to grapple with the problems of rapid growth, for example, the company's quality control procedures were not as effective as they might have been until they were taken in hand. Westwood had reached that classical stage in its development when it was crying out for a more professional approach.

'I could see I was actually stopping the company from progressing,' said Hazlewood. Believing strongly that identifying a problem is three parts of the way towards solving it, Hazlewood decided no half-measures would do. He resolved to take more of a back seat in the running of the company. He handed over the managing directorship to John Derham, his thirty-two-year-old sales director, and promoted his works and purchasing managers to the rank of director. He announced that in future the company would be run by this triumvirate of directors.

Hazlewood remained as chairman, but to underline his resolve to withdraw from the day to day running of the company, he moved to a smaller office away from the centre of operations.

Coinciding with this shift in managerial control, Hazlewood made a magnanimous gesture which left other industrialists aghast. He gave away a quarter of the company's shares to thirty-five of his most loyal employees. 'I was going to give them only ten per cent, but I decided that would be too mean,' he said with an impish grin.

Typically, Hazlewood made the decision to give away the shares on impulse. 'When I came to work in the morning, I had no intention of doing it. I had never thought about it before,' he said. But he did not believe it would have been sufficient to hand over management control without backing it up with a stake in the company. 'I don't think that would have been honest. That was the value I placed on them. They had supported me so fully. I had really been the administrator of their efforts,' he rationalised.

He dismissed any suggestion that he did it as a motivator. 'I have always refused to put carrots down for anybody. These people have always operated without carrots. They never knew what was going to happen.' He did, however, feel that it would give them 'strength' to know that their decisions would now affect the value of their own shareholding.

It was typical of Hazlewood that he divided the shares among the longest-serving and most dedicated employees and not merely among the most senior members of his staff. Although the top three directors share twenty per cent of the company between them, some of the beneficiaries of the remaining five per cent work on the shopfloor.

Hazlewood conceded that there might be some more senior employees who had not been so long with the company who might have felt aggrieved to have been left out in the cold, but he was in no doubt that he had rewarded the right people. 'The others have some more of their apprenticeship to serve,' he said simply.

Under the new management approach, Westwood is being run along more professional lines. The quirky touches of brilliance that have characterised Hazlewood's idiosynchratic style, have no place in managing director Derham's plans. He has, for example, introduced management meetings for the first time. Hazlewood hated group meetings. He much preferred one-to-one discussions, but he acknowledged that his autocratic style had begun to cause problems. 'I'd forget to tell the others what I had discussed with one of the staff and then people would sometimes be working at cross-purposes,' he admitted.

Derham took over determined to run things differently. He set about delegating responsibility down the line and made it clear that middle managers would have a freer hand to operate according to their own ideas provided they met agreed business goals.

He introduced departmental budgets for the first time in the company's history. Before, all the decisions on spending were channelled through Hazlewood, much to the consternation of the finance director. Hazlewood would allocate the amounts to be spent on advertising, for example, according to his own gut feeling.

'If I'm expecting people to take responsibility for their actions, they have to have a system other than talking to me of knowing what's going on,' declared Derham.

He has been cautious, however, to avoid the pendulum swinging too far in the opposite direction. He was anxious that the entrepreneurial flair that had characterised the company for so long should not become bogged down in bureaucratic systems of control. He was keen, too, to adopt an open door policy in his dealings with the staff.

'There always used to be this great fear of going into Gerry's office, which I even experienced myself in the early days,' said Derham. 'Within reason, people can now wander in and out without any worry at all. I've tried to encourage that.'

Stepping back from the day-to-day running of Westwood has given Hazlewood the opportunity to reflect on where his future lies. He originally became an entrepreneur because he was determined to be a millionaire by the time he was forty, an ambition he fulfilled several times over. Whatever role he plays in the company's development, he can be comforted by the knowledge that he has never allowed anything to stand in his path in the past. The road to success for a company that cornered seventy per cent of a market previously dominated by American tractors, has been a far from easy one.

A whole series of disasters in the early days nearly put paid to Hazlewood's aspirations. 'Looking back in hindsight, all of the barriers were me,' he confessed in a typical piece of introspective insight. 'I hate to say it, but that's probably true of any businessman. The thing you'll hear most people say is that they can't do something because they haven't got the money. That just happens to be the most convenient excuse they can find and the one that's acceptable to everyone else. But it's absolutely not true, because if you're doing the right thing the money will appear.'

Hazlewood did not always exude such confidence. As a child, he was shy and retiring and regarded himself as an abject failure. He was constantly in the shadow of his two more successful elder brothers, who shone at school while he was bottom of the class. He hated school so much that he didn't turn up for the final term at the grammar school he just managed to scrape into; instead, he secretly found a job, deceiving his mother by so doing.

When he took up an apprenticeship at a leading engineering company, however, he discovered that he did after all have some talent. To his, and everybody else's surprise, he won the prize for being the best apprentice after six months. But he decided he could not face being behind a machine for the rest of the six-year apprenticeship and he joined his brothers' landscape gardening business in High Wycombe.

His eldest brother, Jeff, who he looked up to as a father figure, suggested he should set up a retail outlet for selling garden machinery to broaden the business. Hazlewood was so inexperienced that when he got his first customer he didn't know how to make out the invoice properly. But he learned fast and discovered that he enjoyed selling.

He eventually did so well that he was making good profits, but these were being drained off by the rest of the market garden business which was struggling to remain viable. Hazlewood decided to buy out his part of the business from his brothers, though he could ill afford it. He found himself in sole charge of a business that had few financial resources and a lot of debts.

Desperately seeking a way out of the crisis, he sought help from a management consulting group, which made no bones about telling him that he was going broke. Undeterred, Hazlewood managed to secure a bank overdraft and paid off his suppliers little by little.

At about that time, he was approached by a customer who had heart trouble and asked if Hazlewood could supply a kick-start mower because the pull-start machines were too much of a strain to operate. Unable to find such a machine on the market, Hazlewood designed his own. 'It started me thinking. If I could make that, perhaps I could make other things. So I made a very small rotary mower, which I bent up in a vice, bought an engine and put it on the machine.'

At first it was a laborious procedure, stamping out and welding the parts by hand. Hazlewood used to work in a small cramped shed at night, running the retail business by day. But the machines sold well and he had soon made enough profit to invest in a £800 tool to stamp out the sheet metal.

Eventually, business was so brisk he needed a factory to operate from. He located an old three-storey converted furniture factory, which was available at a cheap rent. The problem was it was far too large for his embryonic manufacturing operation. He entered into a sub-letting agreement, but the other partner later pulled out, leaving Hazlewood with the crippling costs of running a factory that was far too big for his purposes.

'That was a very difficult period,' recalled Hazlewood. 'I couldn't see how we could possible survive. We were only using a sixth of the factory.' He hung on tenaciously, determined not to seek venture capital. 'That's just what people don't need when they're building a business,' he asserted. 'If you want to give away half your business, that's a good way to do it, but you will still have to solve your own problems. We borrow a lot of money now, but it is borrowed on the success that we've achieved, not on anything artificial.'

Little by little, Hazlewood managed to sub-let parts of the High Wycombe factory and again turned crisis into success. His workforce by now had grown to thirty and he felt ready to launch a sit-on mower which he christened the Lawnbug. It was the precursor of the garden tractors which were later to make such a dramatic penetration of the market place. Garden tractors have larger wheels than sit-on mowers and are more versatile. The cutting blades can be easily removed so that the tractor can perform a whole range of other gardening tasks. Westwood sold the concept in this country by promoting the garden tractor as a fun machine to ride on, which transforms mowing from a chore into a delight.

By 1972 things were going so well for Hazlewood that he found himself in the ironic position of wanting more factory space. But he had by then let most of it out. He searched the country for a larger factory and was finally attracted to Plymouth where the local council offered him a prime three acre site at a low rental.

Hazlewood approached the Department of Trade & Industry for assistance and was offered a £70,000 grant. He felt, after all his financial problems, he had won the pools. But his troubles were about to start all over again.

On the strength of the DTI offer, Hazlewood moved half of his operation into a pilot 10,000 sq ft unit at Plymouth and made preparations to build a much larger factory, using the initial £25,000 of the grant as a deposit. But the early 1970s were boom time and building costs doubled overnight. Hazlewood suddenly found he was expected to put down a £50,000 deposit.

'All of a sudden something that looked like a pools win became an utter disaster,' Hazlewood recalled. 'We had started something and we couldn't stop it. I went to the DTI to explain the problem. All they said was: "Hard luck". I couldn't believe it. For the third time, it looked as though the business was going out of control. The bailiffs were knocking on the door. It's easy to laugh about it now, but at the time it was very worrying. I would have given anything to escape.'

By now, Hazlewood had become a virtual Houdini at escaping financial disaster. He signed an onerous mortgage agreement with the Norwich Union and poured every penny he could lay his hands on into paying for the new factory. The more spacious accommodation gave him the opportunity to spread his wings and go into production in earnest. He became so skilled at driving his American rivals from the British market that a reporter from *Fortune* magazine was despatched to Westwood to explore the secrets of Hazle-wood's success.

It is difficult to find anyone at Westwood who can put his finger precisely on what has accounted for the company's success. 'My first answer would be to say that it was because we decided to do it,' said managing director Derham, who began working for Westwood as a packer on the shopfloor and once shared an interest in scientology with Hazlewood.

Derham accepts, however, that the will to succeed has to be backed up by a marketing strategy. When Westwood first appeared on the scene, American manufacturers seemed to have the market sewn up. At that time, one British distributor was selling around 8,000 US-made tractors a year. Within eight years of Westwood's arrival on the market, the number of US machines had been whittled down to about 200 a year.

In the early days Westwood pushed the fact that its tractors were made specifically for the UK market. It also introduced innovations. The mowing mechanism of the American tractors discharged grass cuttings to the side, which meant that they often ended up in the flower boarders. Westwood's machines discharged the cuttings to the rear, leaving them in neat straight lines. Westwood also introduced a lot of tractor accessories, some of which it gave away to boost sales.

Westwood's policy of self-sufficiency has also played an important part in its growth. Making parts in-house is not necessarily the most cost-effective solution initially. There are operations that have been carried out in the Westwood factory which could almost certainly have been performed more cheaply by an outside contractor. But Derham points out that by gradually perfecting the in-house production processes, Westwood eventually managed to make parts more cheaply than outside contractors and at the same time achieved greater control over its costs.

There have been times, too, when self-sufficiency has led to enormous cost savings. When, some years ago, Hazlewood explored the idea of introducing an automatic paint spraying system at the Westwood factory, there were ready made systems on the market, which the company could easily have afforded. 'Instead of taking the easy route, Gerry personally built the spray system physically himself with the blokes in the factory. It worked extremely well and cost £70,000 less,' recalled Derham.

Before making any business decision, Hazlewood tended to first work out in his mind what it would cost to produce something in-house. He applied the same philosophy to purchasing. Whenever he went to a supplier for components or raw materials, he always had a figure in mind that was often well below what the supplier would be asking. Hazlewood would refuse to give ground and he usually got his own way.

Becoming a back-seat chairman has not meant that Hazlewood's entrepreneurial flair has been lost to Westwood. He now has the time to concentrate on special projects. One such project has grown out of the company's penchant for self-sufficiency. When Westwood began to experiment with robotic welding techniques, it could not find a system on the market that suited its needs, so Hazlewood decided to design his own. He was so pleased with the finished result that he decided to market it to other companies, mainly in the US.

'The system is about three times more productive as any normal system,' claimed Hazlewood. 'Although we had a government grant of £5,000 to develop it, that only covered a third of the cost of the project. It got to the point where we realised it was never going to pay to make it just for ourselves. We decided to take all the experience we had gained from the prototypes we had built and turn that into a marketable product.'

The robot systems are assembled at a 40,000 sq ft factory the company acquired in North Carolina in the US. The factory was originally purchased to produce garden tractors for the US market, but unfavourable exchange rates and a price war among American manufacturers rendered this temporarily unviable.

Hazlewood determined to plough no more than £100,000 into the project. If by then it had not been standing on its own two feet, he would have abandoned it. But orders worth hundreds of thousands of dollars were soon coming in. 'It could easily become much bigger than tractors,' predicted Hazlewood.

Hazlewood has turned self-sufficiency into almost a fetish. When he wanted to make a video of the robot system as a marketing tool, he was horrified at the cost of using professional film makers. So he decided to shoot the eight minute video himself. There was just one snag. He wanted to feature himself in the video explaining the advantages of the system. This presented no obstacle to Hazlewood. He simply shot the video by remote control.

Hazlewood's charismatic personality will clearly continue to play an influential role in the company's future development, despite his more remote position. His characteristic brilliant flashes of lateral thinking are still much in evidence.

Shortly after he stood down as managing director, he arranged for a group of Westwood dealers to be taken on a helicopter trip. The flight was not so much a reward for having sold a lot of garden tractors, but was meant to be something of an eye-opener. Some dealers had suggested that the company might be close to saturation point in its efforts to sell more of the machines on the UK market. This, for virtually a one-product company, represented a serious threat.

To put an end to such defeatist talk, Hazlewood sent the dealers aloft so that they could see at first hand how many gardens there were that were big enough to be in need of the company's tractors. The dealers returned to earth with their horizons widened and a renewed determination to capture even greater market shares.

Hazlewood has been at pains to resist any temptation to interfere in management decisions, however. He and Derham tend to discuss strategic issues on the 'neutral ground' of the golf course. There is an unwritten understanding between them that whatever ideas or suggestions Hazlewood offers, Derham can feel free to take them or leave them.

There's one tradition that Hazlewood does insist on retaining, however. He still regularly mows the grass in the grounds of the company's head office – with a Westwood tractor of course. That way he will never become entirely detached from the product that has made him one of Britain's most successful entrepreneurs.

INDEX